LEARN TO
crochet IN 10 EASY LESSONS

LEARN TO
crochet IN 10 EASY LESSONS

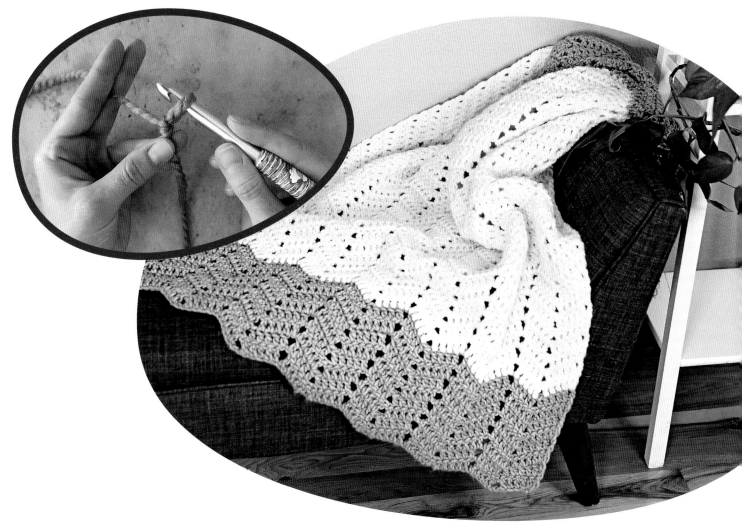

Salena Baca

STACKPOLE BOOKS

Essex, Connecticut
Blue Ridge Summit, Pennsylvania

STACKPOLE BOOKS

An imprint of Globe Pequot, the trade division of The Rowman & Littlefield Publishing Group, Inc.
4501 Forbes Blvd., Ste. 200
Lanham, MD 20706
www.rowman.com

Distributed by NATIONAL BOOK NETWORK
800-462-6420

British Library Cataloguing in Publication Information available

Library of Congress Cataloging-in-Publication Data
Names: Baca, Salena, author.
Title: Learn to crochet in 10 easy lessons / Salena Baca.
Description: First edition. | Essex, Connecticut : Stackpole Books, [2022]
  | Summary: "This book is a complete beginner's guide, broken down into
  easy and manageable steps, to have you crocheting actual items as you
  learn new skills. It starts with the basics of how to choose yarn and
  hooks, and then teaches the basic stitches as well as chart reading,
  before going on to working crochet in rows, rounds, and more"— Provided
  by publisher.
Identifiers: LCCN 2022010175 (print) | LCCN 2022010176 (ebook) | ISBN
  9780811770743 (paperback) | ISBN 9780811770750 (epub)
Subjects: LCSH: Crocheting.
Classification: LCC TT825 .B29367 2022 (print) | LCC TT825 (ebook) | DDC
  746.43/4—dc23/eng/20220318
LC record available at https://lccn.loc.gov/2022010175
LC ebook record available at https://lccn.loc.gov/2022010176

⊖™ The paper used in this publication meets the minimum requirements of American National Standard for Information Sciences—Permanence of Paper for Printed Library Materials, ANSI/NISO Z39.48-1992.

First Edition

contents

introduction

I learned to crochet at the age of five, when my first lessons were to complete projects for school: a case for my flute, some goat horns as a prop for a school play, and granny squares to make blankets for our community.

While I'm so glad my teachers introduced crochet to me in school, I lacked any real knowledge or understanding of the craft—what stitches I was making, how to identify or count them, or how to read patterns. And so I worked on the few basics I had learned without knowing what I was doing or how to advance, all the while thinking that because I'd been crocheting for so long, I must be some kind of expert.

Fast-forward a few decades later, when I began teaching some friends to crochet. After a handful of lessons with me (teaching how I was taught), one friend ventured out and taught herself to read patterns; then she started crocheting things I never thought were possible, such as baby clothes, hats, and flower motifs. I was absolutely blown away. That friend helped me see that even though I had been crocheting for more than twenty years, I didn't really know anything about the craft.

From that moment on, I was obsessed with learning all I could about crochet: the stitches, fabrics, techniques, yarns, and tools available for crochet. Because I didn't know what I didn't know, I tried everything and anything I could; I found blogs, read books, watched videos, and finally taught myself how to read patterns. I was determined to become the expert I already thought I was.

I never stopped teaching friends how to crochet, so the lesson plan I used constantly evolved to make learning as simple and streamlined as possible (for myself and my students). Through my years of learning and teaching, I found a specific way to break down crochet fundamentals in the most basic form, and it truly helps most people learn how to crochet without the guessing and frustrations I went through.

I no longer see myself as a crochet expert, because I now view expertise as a journey. Instead, I'm a lifelong learner who works to ensure that crochet is passed through the generations in better hands than we found it, and I hope this book will be your guide on that same journey!

Welcome to crochet!

Peace + Love + Crochet
Salena Baca

Yarn

Here you will learn everything you need to know about choosing yarn for crochet (without feeling overwhelmed).

Yarn might be the reason you want to learn crochet—it's fantastic! But before you buy every ball, cake, and skein you fall in love with, there are some important things to know to make the most out of every single one. Understanding some basic characteristics about yarn is key when starting your crochet journey, and the yarn label is a great place to start.

■ WHAT IS A YARN LABEL?

The packaging around your yarn—that's a label! Just like a tag on your clothes, the information on a yarn label offers important details about the contents.

Yarn labels vary in style, shape, and size, but there are a few key sections they should have.

Brand and Type

Who made the yarn, and what do they call it? Some yarn companies have dozens of yarns, so the exact yarn name is important, especially if you want to find more of the same yarn or see the difference between yarns from the same company.

Fiber Content

This category lists all the fibers used to make a yarn, up to 100%. Knowing what is in your yarn will help you decide what it would be best used for and how to care for it. There are animal, plant, and synthetic fibers to choose from, and a yarn can be made from one of these elements or a combination of them. Don't overthink this too much. For example, consider the project you want to make and decide which fibers can make the best material for that item.

Yardage

This is the total length of yarn a unit has. If you know how much yarn you're getting in a single unit, you can decide how much you'll need to make a project. A pattern should tell you how much yarn (yardage) you'll need to complete a particular project, so you can work up some simple calculations to get exactly what you need.

Yarn label for Bernat Roving.

Gauge and Hook

Most labels show how many single crochet stitches fit into a 4 in. x 4 in. square and the best hook size to use for the yarn. It is handy to learn the best size hook to use with a particular yarn, but when you're following a pattern, use the hook size suggested for the best results.

Yarn Weight

Weight is a universal term used to describe the thickness of a yarn from 0 (smallest) to 7 (largest). You may see a number or category name here that references the size of a yarn based on this classification system. This information helps to estimate the individual size of a yarn so that it can be paired with patterns and projects.

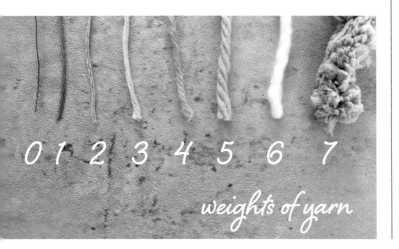

Color and Dye Lot

The label shows the color name and/or number and the batch number in which color was applied. Yarn is dyed in a variety of applications, and each one will look a bit different when you crochet with it! Here are some of the most popular yarn color applications:

Clockwise from top left: solid, marled, multicolored (two samples), and novelty.

Beginner friendly: Solid colors are easier to work with.

- Solid: One unvaried color throughout

Yarn Weight and Hook Sizes

Weight: Number & Class	0 Lace	1 Super Fine	2 Fine	3 Light	4 Medium	5 Bulky	6 Super Bulky	7 Jumbo
Sub-class	• Fingering • 10 Count Thread	• Sock • Fingering • Baby	• Sport • Baby	• DK • Light Worsted	• Worsted • Afghan • Aran	• Chunky • Craft • Rug	• Super Bulky • Roving	• Jumbo • Roving
Hook Size	B-1	B-1 to E-4	E-4 to 7	7 to I-9	I-9 to K-10.5	K-10.5 to M-13	M-13 to Q	Q and larger

*Data shows Craft Yarn Council guidelines, reflecting information collected and shared by industry leaders.

Not beginner friendly: Get comfortable with crochet before working with these colors and textures.

- Marled: Strands of different-colored yarn twisted together
- Multicolored (variegated): Two or more distinct color repeats, in any length of color application
- Novelty: Varying textures, fibers, and colors spun together

Care Instructions

Yarn is a fiber with which fabric is created as you crochet. Based on the fiber contents, the label outlines how best to care for a yarn and the finished projects you make with it. For example, some wool fibers should not go into a washing machine or dryer, some fibers are dry-clean only, and some fibers must be hand washed and laid flat to dry. Label symbols are universal and save space.

Guide to Apparel/Textile Care Symbols

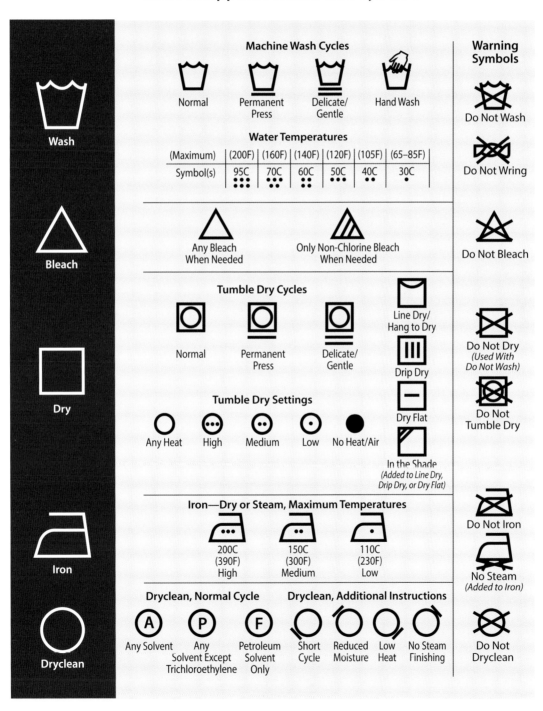

Yarn Units

Yarn is wound and packaged to make it easier to handle and work from. All yarn units have two tail ends to work from. While either may be accessible, you may find that pulling from the center can be a bit messy at first (resulting in yarn barf) but easier once you get going.

You can begin working directly from a yarn unit as soon as you find the end, unless the unit is a hank. Hanks of yarn must be wound into a workable unit (ball, cake, skein) before you can begin to crochet with them.

- **Hank:** For hanks, yarn is wound in a large circle and twisted into shape. Most handmade or dyed yarn is wound this way to help show as much of the color and texture as possible. You can't successfully work directly from this bundle because an untwisted hank does not have any structure to keep from tangling, so it must be wound into a cake, ball, or skein first.

- **Skein:** Industrial machines make skeins, which usually have long bodies.
- **Cake:** Personal yarn winders or industrial machines make cakes of yarn, which are short and wide.
- **Ball:** Balls of yarn that are round are formed by hand. Industrial machines make balls that look like donuts!

turn this hank...

into this cake!

Yarn balls, skeins, and cakes will have a center end and an outside end. You can work from either end. If pulling from the center, you might first see a bit of "yarn barf," but once you get through that initial bit of yarn, you'll have an easier time working through it.

YARN TIPS

- Read your yarn labels! Look for the different sections we outlined and get familiar with the terms and meanings.
- Buy more yarn than you need, especially to get matching dye lots! If a blanket calls for four skeins of yarn, get five skeins just to be sure you have enough.
- Don't toss the label; it tells you everything you need to know about the yarn! When you keep your yarn labels, caring for your finished projects and shopping for refills are much easier.
- Have fun with yarn! Make simple stitch swatches to see how the colors work up and how the fabric feels. It will help you practice crochet and get familiar with the yarn.

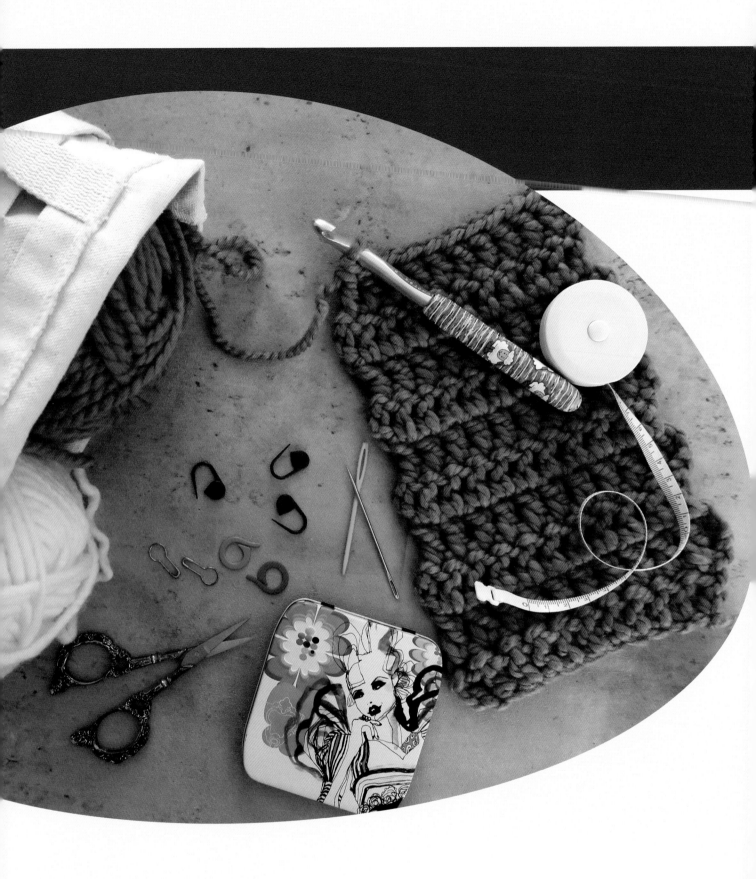

LESSON 2

Tools

Crochet hook—check! But a few other essential tools will help to make crochet more comfortable and successful!

While the most basic tool in crochet is the hook, you might feel overwhelmed when you realize how many brands, sizes, colors, and styles there are to choose from. Learning how to find a good fit, and using just a few other tools when you crochet, can make a huge difference in your experience.

HOOKS

Crochet hooks are the most fundamental tool in crochet; we need them to create stitches and fabric. They come in a variety of sizes, shapes, and materials. Let's explore more about the tool that makes crochet possible.

Size

Crochet hooks are manufactured in universal sizes to work with universal yarn weights (0–7). They are made and measured in millimeters (mm) by diameter and, depending on the manufacturer, may be identified in any combination of letters, numbers, and metric measurements.

Hooks are marked with their individual size, in USA terms with a letter/number, metric terms in millimeters, or a combination of both.

Crochet Hook Size Ranges

Metric	USA	Metric	USA
2.25mm	B-1	6mm	J-10
2.50mm	-	6.5mm	K-10.5
2.75mm	C-2	7mm	-
3.125mm	D	8mm	L-11
3.25mm	D-3	9mm	M/N-13
3.50mm	E-4	10mm	N/P-15
3.75mm	F-5	11.5mm	P-16
4mm	G-6	12mm	-
4.25mm	G	15mm	P/Q
4.50mm	7	15.75mm	Q
5mm	H-8	16mm	Q
5.25mm	I	19mm	S
5.50mm	I-9	25mm	T/U/X
5.75mm	J	30mm	T/X

Data shows Craft Yarn Council guidelines, reflecting information collected and shared by industry leaders.

Anatomy

While styles and brands differ, the general anatomy of crochet hooks is the same. The most important features are the head, lip, and groove, because these are what you'll use to pull up yarn, make loops, and work into fabric. Some heads are made blunt and round, and some are pointy. Grooves can be deep or shallow. Finally, the lip can be long and thin or short and round. You may not know what style or brand hook you like best until you try a few.

Round Head, Short Lip, Shallow Groove

Pointy Head, Long Lip, Deep Groove

There are a variety of styles of crochet hooks, but the basic anatomy is the same.

Material

Crochet hooks can be made from a variety of materials. Each one has a pro and con, depending on the yarn, crochet project, and your own preferences. The most common materials you'll find include the following:

- **Aluminum:** Strong, very durable option. These are typically inexpensive and great for beginners, especially as you try different brands and types when you get started.
- **Plastic:** Flexible, light weight option. These are also great for beginners, because they are very lightweight, which is easier to use with large yarn and can help minimize hand fatigue.

Grips

The handle of a crochet hook can be standard (no extra grip or material) or cased to add bulk, which may be more comfortable as you hold your hook while you work.

■ STITCH MARKERS

Markers are referenced throughout this book, and for good reason! These little tools help mark the tops of stitches, so you'll learn how to count them properly. While proper stitch markers exist, you can use other household items like paper clips, safety pins, or bobby pins if you prefer.

While hooks are often made of aluminum or plastic, their handles may include other materials, and the grip is sometimes thicker for comfort.

Stitch markers come in handy for marking individual stitches and rows of work.

A basic crochet toolkit should include hooks, stitch markers, measuring tape, a yarn needle, and scissors.

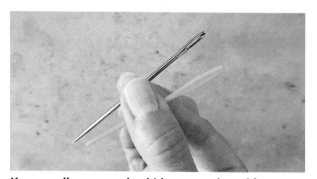

Yarn needles are used to hide yarn ends and for sewing pieces of crochet together.

OTHER HANDY CROCHET TOOLS

Needles
When choosing yarn needles, the size of the eye determines the largest size of yarn you can work with. Pointy tips are for sewing, and blunt tips are best for weaving.

Scissors
Scissors should be sharp, especially to cut yarn without fraying it.

Measuring Tape
A fabric measuring tape that is also retractable is quick and easy to use.

Notions Tin
Tins can hold needles, stitch markers, and other small notions all in one place.

Pencil Case
These are the perfect length and size for holding crochet hooks and scissors.

Project Bags and Baskets
If you have a project that you want to take on the go, bags are best! Baskets are great for storing projects around the house.

TOOL TIPS

- Try a few different hook brands until you find ones that you're most comfortable with.
- When you're just starting out, you may not know what you like until you start to crochet.
- Always use stitch markers!

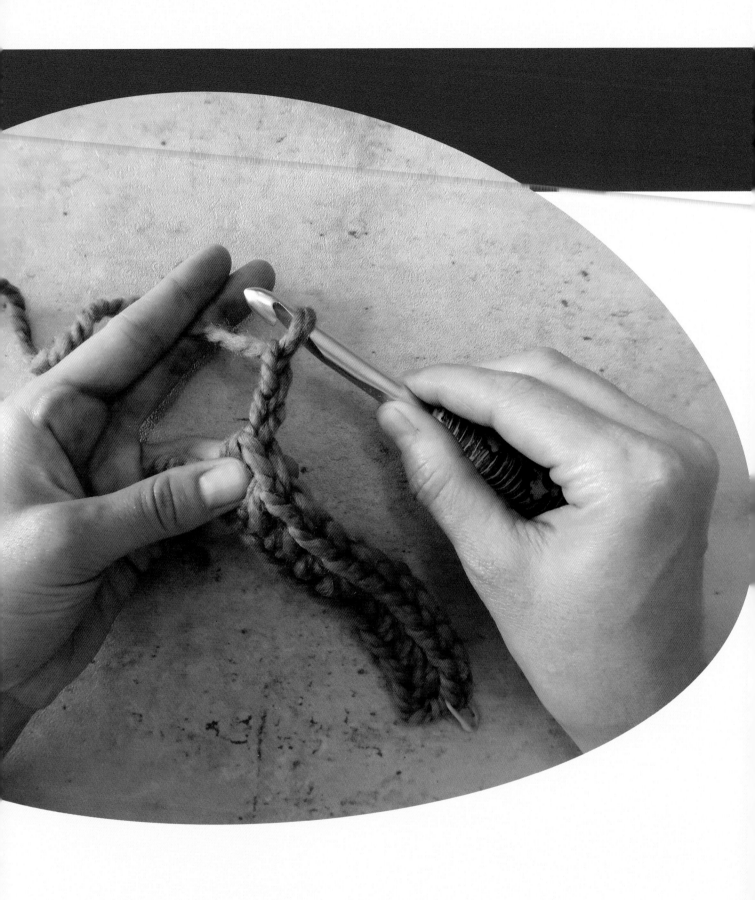

LESSON 3

Stitches

Before you can crochet all of the things, get a solid foundation by learning the basic stitches!

Whether you're brand new to crochet or know a stitch or two, this is a section you should put a lot of effort into. Here, we're finally picking up a hook to work basic crochet stitches, and it's important to really learn the look and feel of each one. Every stitch is complete with a photo tutorial, written pattern, and diagram so that you will be able to learn more than just stitches.

While the instructions and diagrams in this section are for beginners to learn and follow, you can skip ahead to Lesson 4 if you need more information about pattern reading.

WORKING IN ROWS

Working rows of stitches is the easiest way to learn each stitch—and the best way to learn how to crochet. Before you can begin working crochet projects, this section concentrates on the step-by-step process of creating stitches so that you can identify and count each one with ease and confidence.

In this section, you'll learn to create basic stitches by making a swatch (a small piece of fabric) for each one. Follow these tips to get started:

- **Use stitch markers, especially where indicated at the beginning of each row.** This will help you identify the top of the first stitch in each row, which is useful when counting and identifying individual stitches.
- **Ignore the beginning chains.** Individual patterns should always note whether a beginning (turning) chain counts as a stitch. For the purpose of learning how to create and count each stitch, beginning chains in this section are worked merely to create stitch height and will not be counted as the first stitch. The general rule is: 1 chain = single

crochet, 2 chains = half double crochet, 3 chains = double crochet.

- **Use thick yarn and a big hook.** This section helps you practice the technical side of crochet, so choosing an economical yarn to use here is best. Try a light color yarn in the weight 5 category and pair it with a 6–9 mm (J-10, K-10½, L-11, or M/N-13) crochet hook. The larger hook and yarn will help you to feel comfortable holding a hook and yarn, and the stitches and fabric you create will be big enough to identify and count.
- **Don't stress; have fun!** Crochet requires your eyes, brain, fingers, hands, arms, shoulders, and back to work together, so it can be a bit tricky to grasp at first. Crochet can feel awkward, and that's normal—you're using both hands to create fabric with yarn. Work each stitch slowly, take your time, take breaks, stretch a lot, and enjoy!

SLIPKNOT

Slipknots are not stitches, and they don't count as stitches. The loop formed is used to attach yarn to the hook so you can begin to crochet stitches.

1. Cross yarn tail over ball yarn.

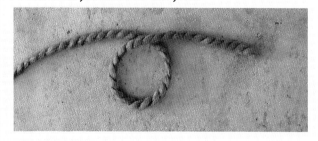

2. Cross ball yarn over center.

3. Pull ball yarn through circle.

4. Pull until knot forms.

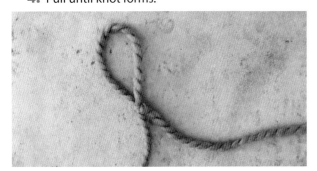

5. Put loop on hook and adjust.

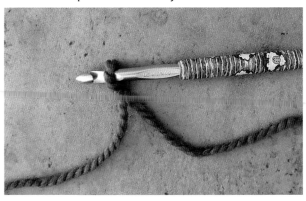

SLIPKNOT TIPS

- Once formed, the loop is adjustable (can be made larger or smaller).
- Loop should slide across hook (not too tight or too loose).
- This loop never counts as a stitch; it is simply how yarn is attached to the hook.

Practice: Work the slipknot a few times until you can create it quickly without thinking.

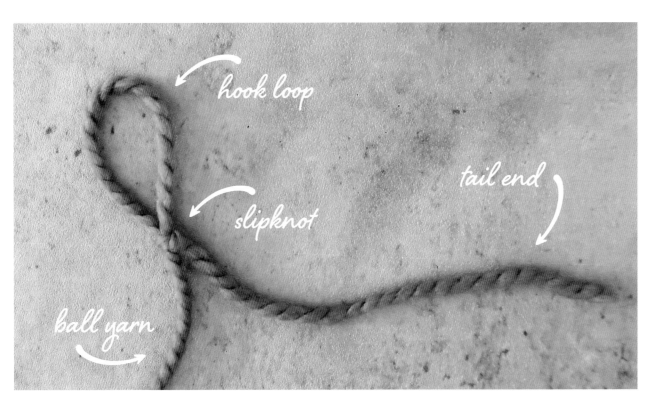

■ HOLDING YOUR YARN AND HOOK

When you learn to crochet, you're learning a lot all at once. You're learning to hold a crochet hook and yarn with both hands and to work projects by creating lots of individual stitches. Crochet can be awkward at first, and that's okay. It takes time and practice.

Right- or Left-Handed

Nearly all crochet patterns are written for right-handed people (that means the crochet hook is held in the right hand, and stitches are worked from right to left). Left-handed people can work many patterns—those that are symmetrical and have no special shaping—simply by following the instructions as written, holding the hook in their left hand and working stitches from left to right. That is the case with all of the patterns in this book.

Holding Styles

There is no one right way to hold your crochet hook or your yarn. As long as you're not adjusting after each stitch, and your hands and shoulders aren't too tense, you've got a comfortable style. However, here are two popular ways to hold a crochet hook:

Right-handed hook hold

Pencil hold

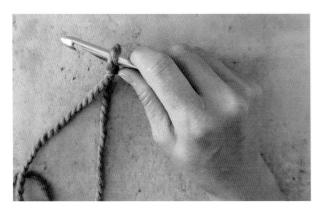

Knife hold

Right-handed yarn hold

Pinch yarn between pointer, middle fingers

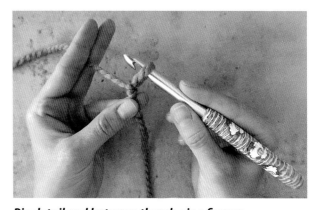

Pinch tail end between thumb, ring fingers

Left-handed hook hold

Pencil hold

Knife hold

Left-handed yarn hold

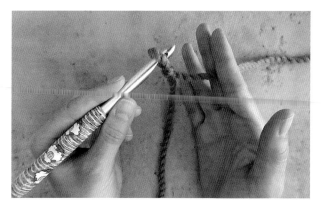

Pinch yarn between pointer, middle fingers

Pinch tail end between thumb, ring fingers

HOLDING TIP

When you're a beginner, hold the crochet hook and yarn in one of these styles until you find what works most comfortably and naturally for you.

Practice: As you start to learn and practice crochet stitches, be mindful of how you're holding your yarn and hook each time, and adjust until you find what is most comfortable.

CHAIN

The chain is the first stitch you'll learn to crochet. It is the foundation used to learn and work all the other stitches in this section.

1. Start with a slipknot on the hook; hold the hook and yarn in a comfortable position.

2. Wrap the yarn around the hook from the bottom and around the top; this is called a "yarn over hook."

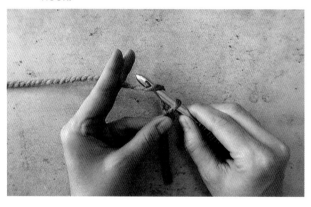

3. Use the hook to pull the yarn through the loop on the hook.

4. One chain has been formed.

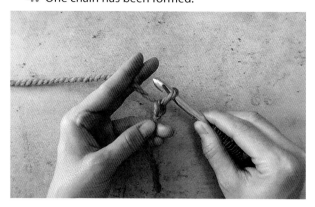

5. Continue to yarn over and pull the yarn through the loop on the hook for the number of chains needed. In this photo, 10 chains have been made.

Stitch Pattern Chart and Practice

Chain Stitch Diagram. To work from this diagram, you will form a slipknot, chain 10, and fasten off (see page 17).

Stitch Key ⬯ Chain

How to Count Chain Stitches

Every stitch in crochet has a front and back. As you create a stitch, the fabric you can see is the front, and the fabric on the other side is the back. Each side looks very different and will create different-looking fabric. It is important to note these two sides so that you can learn to count individual stitches and create fabric that intentionally shows the front for certain projects.

- **From the front:** Each chain has a front and back loop, which look like hearts.
- **From the back:** The front and back loops are visible on the top and bottom of a center loop.

CHAIN TIPS

- The more you practice, the more even your stitches will look and the faster you'll work!
- If you get frustrated, put your work down and come back to it.
- The crochet hook should be facing downward, not sideways or up, so that it can freely move through the loop on your hook.
- Hold the last chain formed to keep your work steady before creating the next chain.

Practice: Follow the stitch pattern at least five complete times. Don't rip out your first chain so you can keep track of your progress!

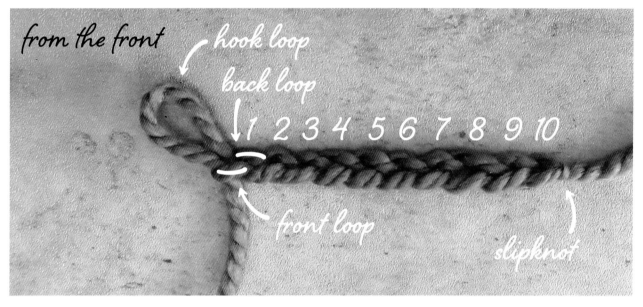

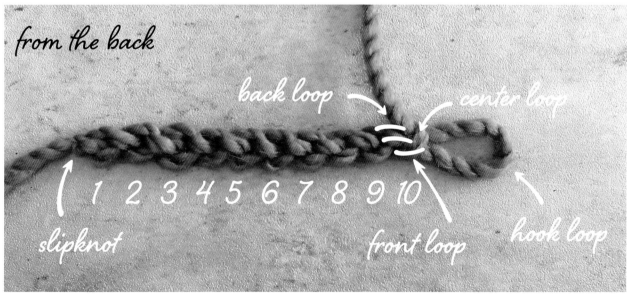

FASTENING OFF

When you've completed a project, you'll detach your project from the yarn and form a knot so that it doesn't unravel. When a pattern tells you to fasten off, this is what you'll do:

1. Cut yarn at least 10 in. (25 cm) from loop on hook.
2. Pull yarn tail through loop on hook until a knot forms.

SINGLE CROCHET

The single crochet is a small stitch, with very few motions to complete it. However, the size makes it a bit difficult to identify. If you struggle with this stitch, move on to the half double and double crochet stitches, and then try this one last!

1. Chain 11.

2. Work into back of chain. Skip 1 chain.

3. Insert hook below center loop.

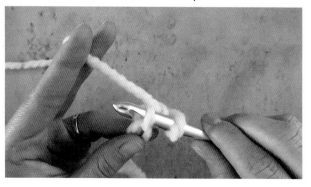

4. Yarn over hook.

5. Pull yarn through center loop.

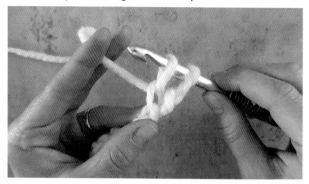

6. Yarn over hook.

7. Pull yarn through two loops on hook. One single crochet made.

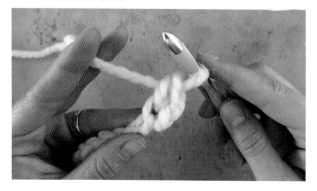

8. Place a stitch marker on both loops at the top of this stitch.

9. Repeat steps 3 through 7 for each chain. When Row 1 is complete, you'll have 10 single crochet stitches.

10. Begin Row 2: Chain 1.

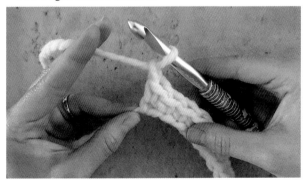

11. Turn your work. Skip 1 chain.

12. Insert hook below both loops of stitch.

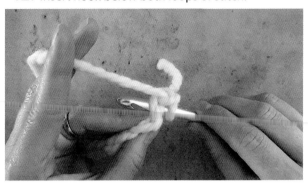

13. Yarn over hook.

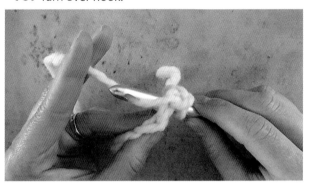

14. Pull yarn through both loops.

15. Yarn over hook.

16. Pull yarn through both loops on hook. One single crochet made.

Note: Place a stitch marker on both loops at the top of this stitch.

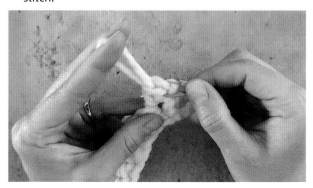

17. Repeat steps 12 through 16 for each stitch across the row. When Row 2 is complete, you'll have 10 single crochet stitches.

Stitch Pattern Chart and Practice

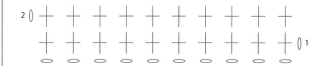

Single Crochet Stitch Diagram

Stitch Key   ⊂⊃ Chain

              ╋ Single Crochet

To work from this diagram, form a slipknot, chain 11.

Row 1: Skip 1 chain (not a stitch), single crochet into second chain from hook (place stitch marker into top of stitch), work 1 single crochet into each chain across—10 single crochet.

Row 2: Chain 1 (not a stitch), turn, single crochet into first stitch (place stitch marker into top of stitch), work 1 single crochet into each stitch across—10 single crochet.

Repeat Row 2 until 10 rows are complete; fasten off.

Ten rows of single crochet complete.

How to Count Single Crochet Stitches
- **From the front:** Just under the front loop, two strands of yarn form a V.
- **From the back:** Just under the back loop, there is a horizontal bar and an upside-down V.
- **From the top:** Every stitch looks like the front of a chain stitch (little hearts).

from the top

SINGLE CROCHET TIPS

- This is a tight, dense stitch, and the fabric it creates will curl (that's okay).
- Use a stitch marker as you create your first stitch in each row.
- Count stitches after every row to make sure your stitch count is right, before you begin the next row.

Practice: Follow the stitch pattern at least 5 complete times. Don't rip out your first single crochet swatch, so that you keep track of your progress!

from the front

hook loop

top of first stitch

1 2 3 4 5 6 7 8 9 10

1 2 3 4 5 6 7 8 9 10

slipknot

chain 1 (not a stitch)

from the back

hook loop

top of first stitch

1 2 3 4 5 6 7 8 9

chain 1 (not a stitch)

1 2 3 4 5 6 7 8 9 10

slipknot

HALF DOUBLE CROCHET

The half double crochet has a few more steps than the single crochet. It's a taller and wider stitch to create.

1. Chain 12.

2. Work into back of chain. Skip 2 chains.

3. Yarn over hook.

4. Insert hook below center loop.

5. Yarn over hook.

6. Pull yarn through center loop.

7. Yarn over hook.

8. Pull yarn through 3 loops on hook; 1 half double crochet complete.

9. Place a stitch marker on both loops at the top of this stitch.

10. Repeat steps 3 through 8 for each chain. When Row 1 is complete, you'll have 10 half double crochet stitches.

11. Begin Row 2: Chain 2. Turn, skip 2 chains.

12. Yarn over hook, find both loops of next stitch.

13. Insert hook below both loops.

14. Yarn over hook.

15. Pull yarn through both loops.

16. Yarn over hook.

17. Pull yarn through 3 loops on hook; 1 half double crochet complete.

18. Place a stitch marker on both loops at the top of this stitch.

19. Repeat steps 12 (except you won't have chains to skip) through 17 for each stitch. When Row 2 is complete, you'll have 10 half double crochet stitches.

Stitch Pattern Chart and Practice

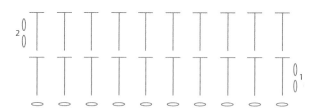

Half Double Crochet Stitch Diagram

Stitch Key   ⬭ Chain

               ⊤ Half Double Crochet

To work from this diagram, form a slipknot, chain 12.

Row 1: Skip 2 chains (not a stitch), half double crochet into third chain from hook (place stitch marker into top of stitch), work 1 half double crochet into each chain across—10 half double crochet.

Row 2: Chain 2 (not a stitch), turn, half double crochet into first stitch (place stitch marker into top of stitch), work 1 half double crochet into each stitch across—10 half double crochet.

Repeat Row 2 until 10 rows are complete, fasten off.

Ten rows of half double crochet complete

How to Count Half Double Crochet Stitches

- **From the front:** Just under the front loop, three strands of yarn begin in the upper left corner and spread out toward the lower right corner.
- **From the back:** Just under the back loop, two strands of yarn horizontally slant to the left, and then two strands of yarn form a V.
- **From the top:** Every stitch looks like the front of a chain stitch (little hearts).

from the top

HALF DOUBLE CROCHET TIPS

- Use a stitch marker as you create your first stitch in each row.
- Count stitches after every row to make sure your stitch count is right, before you begin the next row.

Practice: Follow the stitch pattern at least 5 complete times. Don't rip out your first half double crochet swatch, so that you keep track of your progress!

from the front   *hook loop*   *top of first stitch*

1 2 3 4 5 6 7 8 9 10

1 2 3 4 5 6 7 8 9 10
slipknot   *chain 2 (not a stitch)*

from the back   *hook loop*

top of first stitch   1 2 3 4 5 6 7 8 9 10

chain 2 (not a stitch)   1 2 3 4 5 6 7 8 9 10   *slipknot*

DOUBLE CROCHET

The double crochet is the tallest stitch, with the most steps to complete it. There is noticeable space between each double crochet stitch, which may make each one easier to identify and count.

1. Chain 13.

2. Work into back of chain. Skip 3 chains.

3. Yarn over hook.

4. Insert hook below center loop.

5. Yarn over hook.

6. Pull yarn through center loop.

7. Yarn over hook.

8. Pull yarn through 2 loops on hook.

9. Yarn over hook.

10. Pull through 2 loops on hook; 1 double crochet made.

11. Place a stitch marker on both loops at the top of this stitch.

12. Repeat steps 3 through 10 for each chain. When Row 1 is complete, you'll have 10 double crochet stitches.

13. Begin Row 2: Chain 3, turn, skip 3 chains.

14. Yarn over hook.

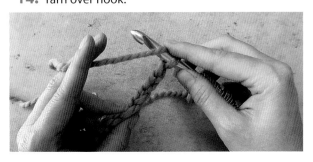

15. Find both loops of next stitch, insert hook below both loops.

16. Yarn over hook.

17. Pull yarn through both loops.

18. Yarn over hook.

19. Pull yarn through 2 loops on hook.

20. Yarn over hook.

21. Pull yarn through 2 loops on hook; 1 double crochet made.

22. Place a stitch marker on both loops at the top of this stitch.

23. Repeat steps 14 (except you won't have chains to skip) through 21 for each stitch. When Row 2 is complete, you'll have 10 double crochet stitches.

Stitch Pattern Chart and Practice

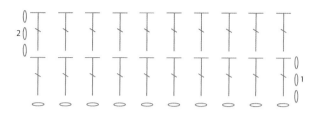

Double Crochet Stitch Diagram

Stitch Key ⬭ Chain

Double Crochet

This diagram indicates to form a slipknot, chain 13.
Row 1: Skip 3 chains (not a stitch), double crochet into fourth chain from hook (place stitch marker into top of stitch), work 1 double crochet into each chain across—10 double crochet.
Row 2: Chain 3 (not a stitch), turn, double crochet into first stitch (place stitch marker into top of stitch), work 1 double crochet into each stitch across—10 double crochet.
Repeat Row 2 until 10 rows are complete, fasten off.

Ten rows of double crochet complete.

How to Count Double Crochet Stitches

- **From the front:** Just under the front loop, two strands of yarn form a V, and then two more strands form an upside-down V.
- **From the back:** One strand of yarn is parallel to the back loop, and 2 additional strands of yarn are perpendicular, forming a I. One strand of yarn sticks out on the left, like a stick person waving with one hand.
- **From the top:** Every stitch looks like the front of a chain stitch (little hearts).

from the top

DOUBLE CROCHET TIPS

- Use a stitch marker as you create your first stitch in each row.
- Count stitches after every row to make sure your stitch count is right before you begin the next row.

Practice: Follow the stitch pattern at least five complete times. Don't rip out your first double crochet swatch so that you can keep track of your progress.

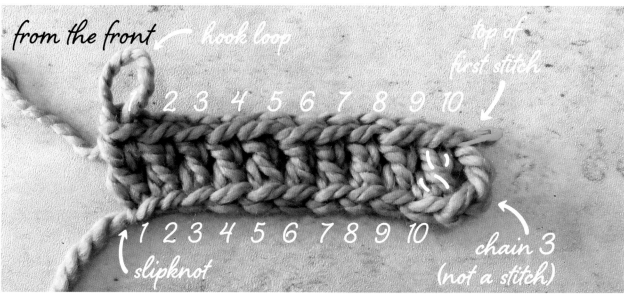

from the front *hook loop* *top of first stitch*

1 2 3 4 5 6 7 8 9 10

1 2 3 4 5 6 7 8 9 10

slipknot *chain 3 (not a stitch)*

from the back *hook loop*

top of first stitch 1 2 3 4 5 6 7 8 9 10

1 2 3 4 5 6 7 8 9 10

chain 3 (not a stitch) *slipknot*

Pattern Reading

Learn how to read and follow written crochet instructions, symbols, and diagrams.

If crochet patterns seem like a strange language, you're not crazy! Crochet instructions are condensed with abbreviations, formatted to follow certain standards, and use mathematical rules to make reading them at a glance more clear. When you understand the formats and terms, you'll be reading and following crochet patterns with ease.

Let's review the pattern sections you'll typically see; use the sample Bobble Stitch Washcloth pattern as shown on page 30 as a reference.

Bobble Stitch Washcloth

BOBBLE STITCH WASHCLOTH

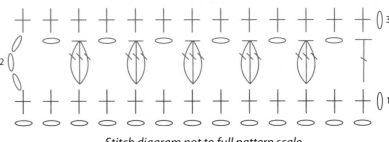

The bobble is a complex stitch that creates a lot of texture and bulk. This two-row repeat gives each side of the fabric a slightly different look.

SIZES/FINISHED MEASUREMENTS
7.5 in. wide x 8 in. tall (19.05 cm x 20.32 cm)

YARN
Knit Picks CotLin DK, Light weight #3 (70% Tanguis cotton, 30% linen; 123 yd./112 m; 1.76 oz./50 g skein):
- Sagebrush: 1 skein

Also try: Lily Sugar 'n Cream, I Love This Cotton, Bernat Handicrafter

HOOK & OTHER MATERIALS
- US size G-6 (4.0 mm) crochet hook
- Scissors
- Yarn needle
- Measuring tape

GAUGE
Gauge is not crucial for this project.

STITCH KEY
ch = chain
sc = single crochet
dc = double crochet

SPECIALTY STITCHES/TECHNIQUES
Bobble = [Yarn over, insert hook into 1 stitch, yarn over, pull back through stitch, yarn over, pull through 2 loops on hook] 4 times total, yarn over, pull through all 5 loops on hook.

■ INSTRUCTIONS
With Sagebrush, ch 32.
Row 1: Skip 1 ch (not a st), work 1 sc into each ch across—31 sc.
Row 2 (right side): Ch 4 (first dc + ch-1 space), turn, skip 1 st, [Bobble, ch 1, skip 1 st] 14 times, dc into last st of row—31 sts; 2 dc + 15 ch + 14 Bobbles.
Row 3: Ch 1 (not a st), turn, work 1 sc into each st across—31 sc.
Repeat Rows 2 and 3 until 21 rows complete (ending on a Row 3 repeat). Fasten off.
Sew in all ends and trim excess.

Stitch Key

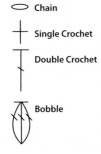

Chain
Single Crochet
Double Crochet
Bobble

Bobble Stitch Washcloth Stitch Pattern

Stitch diagram not to full pattern scale.

PRE-INSTRUCTION SECTION

Crochet patterns typically follow a standard format to make them easy to read, evaluate, and complete. Before the pattern instructions is a section I like to call the "cover page," which outlines what you're making, with what, and how. A cover page may be on a separate page, but it doesn't have to be.

Think of this section like the ingredient and technique list before a recipe. Depending on the publisher, patterns may have different formats, section titles, or verbiage than shown here, with sections like Yarn, Hook, Gauge, Size, and Stitch Key. Reading a pattern means you can evaluate it (sections, flow, terms, instructions) and follow it.

Before you pick up your hook, be sure you have a good understanding of all that is required. Research anything you're not familiar with so that you know what you need to do to successfully work a pattern.

Here are the sections you'll find while working the patterns in this book.

Yarn

This section tells you exactly what yarn was used to create the finished project: brand, type, weight, yardage, amount used, and colors. Yarn alternatives might be suggested here too. If not, you can find substitutes based on the details provided.

Materials

Lists crochet tools and other notions used to complete a project, such as hook size, scissors, tape measure, yarn needle, and stitch markers, to name a few.

Gauge

In crochet, this is a measurement of the stitches per inch (cm) and rows per inch (cm), typically shown over a 4 in. x 4 in. square (10 cm x 10 cm). If the size of a project matters, then the gauge (size) of your stitches and fabric will matter, and you'll want your stitches and fabric to match the pattern gauge.

Size

This section lists the finished dimensions of a project that you can make from the pattern instructions.

Stitch and Term Key

To condense space, crochet stitches are listed in abbreviated form. This section is crucial when following instructions, because basic stitches (and some crochet terms) used within a pattern will be outlined here.

For example, the instructions for a double crochet stitch written out would look like this: *Yarn over, insert hook into 1 stitch, yarn over, pull through stitch, yarn over, pull through 2 loops on hook, yarn over, pull through 2 loops on hook.*

Instead of using this statement over and over again within a pattern, the stitch will be listed in the Stitch Key with its abbreviation (dc), and you'll see simply dc within the instructions. Then every time you see dc within the instructions, you'll know what to do!

COMMON ABBREVIATIONS

Abbreviation	Stitch or Description
ch	chain
cm	centimeters
Color A (B, C . . .)	yarn color assignment
dc	double crochet
hdc	half double crochet
mm	millimeters
oz.	ounces
RS	right side
sc	single crochet
sl st	slip stitch
st(s)	stitch(es)
WS	wrong side
yd.	yards

Crochet abbreviations are listed for reference in US terms. Individual patterns should define any stitches and abbreviations used if a universal definition does not exist.

Specialty Stitch Key

These are combinations of standard stitches, often requiring instructions to complete them. These are abbreviated to shorten the instructions, making them simpler to read and follow.

For example, the instructions for a Bobble stitch written out would be: *[Yarn over, insert hook into 1 stitch, yarn over, pull back through stitch, yarn over, pull through 2 loops on hook] 4 times total, yarn over, pull through all 5 loops on hook.*

Instead of using this statement over and over again within a pattern, the stitch is listed in the Specialty Stitch section with a term (Bobble), and you'll simply see Bobble within the pattern instructions. Then every time you see Bobble within the instructions, you'll know what to do!

SPECIALTY STITCH KEY

Term	Definition
Bobble	All stitches joined at one base and at the top. Try with long stitches, such as double crochet.
Cluster	All stitches have a different base but are joined at the top, decreasing the number of stitches. Try with any stitch: single, half double, or double.
Popcorn	All stitches are joined at one base and at the top. Formed by joining tops of first and last stitch together. Try with double crochet.
Puff	All stitches are joined at one base and at the top. However, this look is only formed with the half double crochet (try it to see)!

Technique Key

This section defines a particular way to work or complete something in crochet, and you'll likely see it bundled together with the Specialty Stitches section. Some examples include the following:

- Where to place a stitch (BLO = Back Loop Only)
- What to do with stitches (dc2tog = double crochet 2 stitches together)

To have a better understanding of stitch placement for this section, remember what you learned about stitch anatomy for the chain, single, half double, and double crochet stitches in Lesson 3:

- Stitches have a front and back side.
- Stitches have a front and back loop on their tops (looks like the chain stitch).
- Stitches have a body length that varies in size (single = smallest, half double = medium, double = tallest).

If a pattern does not specify a special placement or technique for a stitch, always work into the front and back loops on the tops of previous stitches (just as you did when you learned each stitch in Lesson 3).

For example, you might see a chain or group of chains and wonder what to do. Don't complicate it; unless your pattern says otherwise (with a specialty stitch or technique), look for the tops of the chain (front and back loops), and work stitches into both of those loops.

SPECIALTY TECHNIQUE KEY

Abbreviation	Technique
BLO	back loop only
BP	back post
FLO	front loop only
FP	front post
St(X)tog (e.g., sc2tog)	decrease X number of stitches together

Not all patterns work one stitch into one stitch or space. You might see instructions that say to skip one or more stitches (like the Tiny Square Washcloth in Lesson 6), or add more than one stitch into a single stitch or space between stitches (like Silt Stitch Washcloth in Lesson 6). Just pay careful attention to any additional instructions about what you should do and where you should place each stitch you work.

Other specialty stitch placement techniques you may see are:

BLO = back loop only. The back loop is the top loop of the stitch that is farthest from you; BLO means you'll work into the "back loop only," leaving the front loop unworked and exposed.

FLO = front loop only. The front loop is the top loop of the stitch that is closest to you; FLO means you'll work into the "front loop only," leaving the back loop unworked and exposed.

BP = back post. This means you'll work around the post of a stitch from the back side, inserting the hook from the back, around the front of the post, and to the back again.

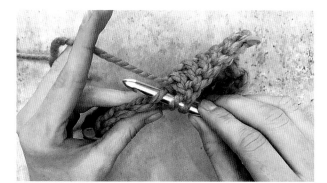

FP = front post. This means you'll work around the post of a stitch from the front side, inserting the hook from the front, around the back of the post, and to the front again.

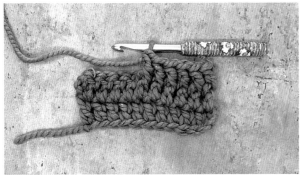

Notes

This section outlines any additional instructions or tips to help you complete a pattern and that might be crucial to understand how a design is worked. For example:

- Hat is worked in rows and then seamed to form a tube.
- Gauge is not crucial.
- Bottom is worked in rows; sides are worked in joined rounds.

Instructions

After the cover page are the instructions. These are the step-by-step directions you'll follow to complete a project. The formatting of this section can be straightforward, but the wording deserves some special attention to understand.

Rows and Rounds: Crochet is worked in rows or rounds. Each row or round is identified with a separate line of instructions and numbered in order of operation.

- **Rows** are worked back and forth, typically in a straight line.
- **Rounds** are worked in a circle or tube and can be joined or worked continuously.

Repeats: These help shorten the amount of instructions needed, similar to a math equation.

In crochet, three distinct characters tell how instructions should be followed.

- **Asterisk:** * = Repeat entire section of instructions between asterisks, as indicated.
- **Brackets: [ ]** = Repeat entire section of instructions between brackets a certain number of times.
- **Parentheses: ( )** = Instructions are worked together into one stitch or space.

Stitch Counts: Final stitch counts should be listed after each row or round of instructions as a means of checking the accuracy of the instructions. You can also use the end stitch count to double-check your stitch work.

In crochet, the beginning (turning) chain is the only place within a pattern that may or may not count as a stitch. A pattern should always identify this point clearly. To help track your stitch counts, use a stitch marker in the top of your first stitch of each row or round.

■ DIAGRAMS

Crochet diagrams are a universal language. Here, crochet stitches and techniques are represented by symbols to give a visual representation of the instructions needed to complete a project. While this book includes diagrams to visualize written instructions, including them with patterns is not typically a common resource.

Key

Just like a map, diagrams should have a key to define each symbol's meaning. Most symbols look just like the crochet stitch or technique they represent!

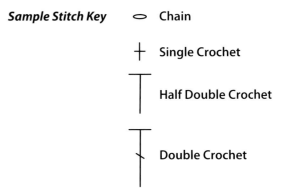

Sample Stitch Key   ⌒ Chain

+ Single Crochet

Half Double Crochet

Double Crochet

How to Read a Diagram

- Determine the starting point: center for circles, bottom for rows.
- Follow diagrams from the bottom up for rows: right to left for odd rows, left to right for even rows.
- Follow diagrams from the center out for circles: Look for beginning chains and follow each symbol counter-clockwise.
- Note join locations for circles and rounds and stopping points for rows.
- Count each stitch per round or row, and make sure your stitch work matches the diagram and written instructions (if provided).

PATTERN TIPS

- When you're new to reading and following patterns, use the suggested yarn weight and size for best results.
- A well-written pattern will outline each abbreviation in the stitch or technique keys, including terms and definitions for specialty stitches and techniques.
- Before you pick up your hook, read through the entire pattern to make sure it is clear and that you can visualize what is required to complete it.

Sample Stitch Diagrams

Stitch Key

⬭	Chain
+	Single Crochet
┬	Double Crochet
⬥	Bobble

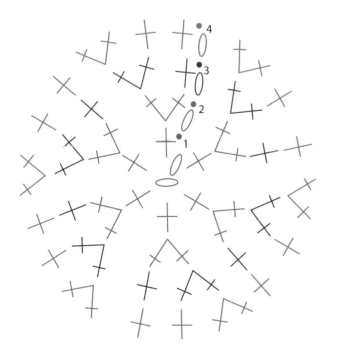

Stitch Key

⬭	Chain
●	Slip Stitch
+	Single Crochet
⋏	2 Single Crochet into 1 Stitch

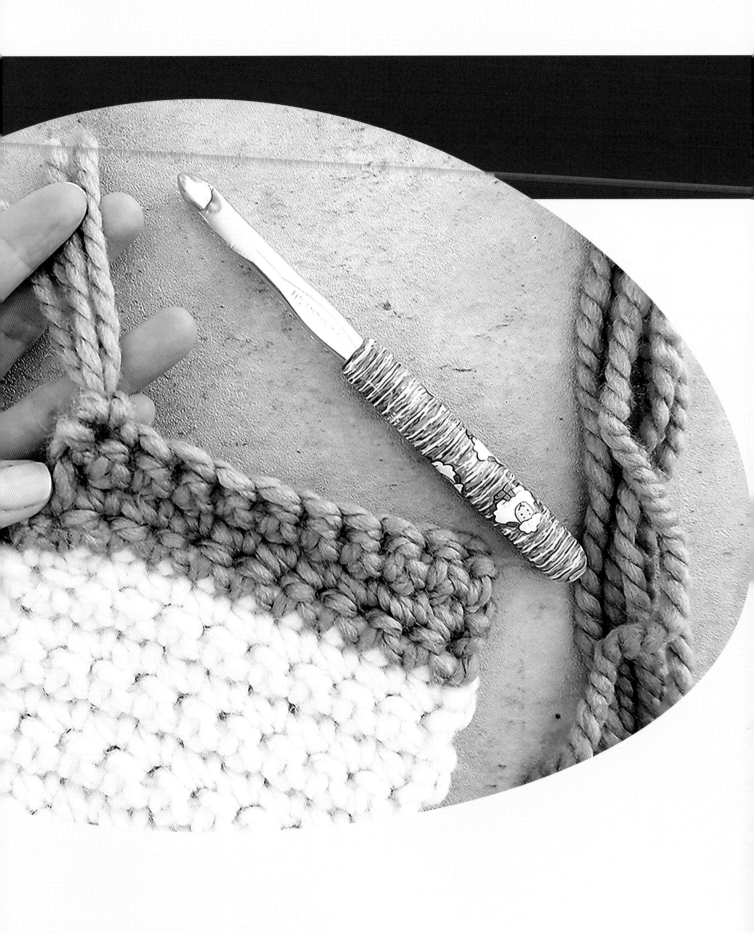

Basic Techniques

In crochet, techniques are categorized as particular ways of performing tasks. Most techniques you can apply will make the crochet projects you create more varied, polished, and functional. There are lots of creative techniques in crochet, with more than one way to perform each one.

This section shares some of the most common techniques in crochet, with the simplest ways to perform them. Before you start your first crochet project, take some time with this section to practice and get comfortable with each concept.

■ YARN ENDS

Every project you crochet will have yarn ends that have to be managed. While beginning and ending tail ends of yarn are typically knotted (fastened off), they should be secured into your crochet fabric in some way to finish off your project. And when you have extra yarn ends because of a color change or new yarn addition, making sure those are secure will help keep your project from unraveling.

TIPS

- Use your single, half double, and double stitch swatches from the previous lesson to practice each technique.
- If you haven't built a crochet toolbox yet, this section is a great opportunity to add yarn needles, scissors, and a tape measure to your stock.
- This is a great section to test out different yarn colors, types, and textures, especially to learn more about the look, feel, gauge, and size of the fabrics you create.

Weaving

1. Thread blunt needle with yarn.

2. Weave needle around yarn strands (not into).

Sewing

1. Thread sharp needle with yarn.

2. Insert needle into yarn strands (sew) to secure.

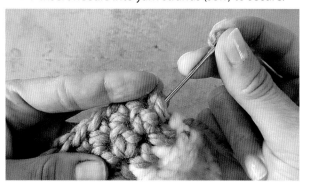

TIPS ON YARN ENDS

- Depending on the yarn you're using, and the project you're creating, yarn ends can be sewn or woven into your crochet fabric. If a pattern doesn't specify, use your best judgment.
- Typically, metal needles are best for sewing, because they have sharp ends. Plastic needles are best for weaving, because they are flexible with blunt ends.
- The eye of your yarn needle should be large enough to thread the yarn you're using.
- Whether weaving or sewing, work in a zigzag pattern to make sure yarn ends are really secure!

CHANGING COLORS

Changing colors is one of the simplest things you can do to adjust the look of a crochet project. After you learn the technique, you can typically change colors any time you want within a project. This technique is also the best way to add a new yarn to a project, especially as you run out of one unit and need to add another.

1. Working any stitch, stop before the final yarn over.

2. Work the final yarn over by pulling the new color through the loop(s).

3. Continue working the pattern and stitches as written.

4. Fasten off tail ends with at least 10 in. (25.4 cm) of length.

5. Knot tail ends together securely with two or three knots.

6. Leave tail ends long for sewing or weaving in later.

TIP

Make sure each tail end of yarn is long enough to knot together, weave, or sew down later on. Yarn ends should be a few times longer than the yarn needle you'll use so that you can easily thread and work with them.

FRINGE

Fringe is not a necessary function of crochet, but it is a really fun and flashy way to finish a project (like the table runner [Lesson 7], wrap [Lesson 7], and banner [Lesson 10] patterns in this book). If you don't love the look of fringe (or the extra work to create and attach it), you can absolutely ignore this finishing technique.

1. Cut a cardboard rectangle measuring fringe length.

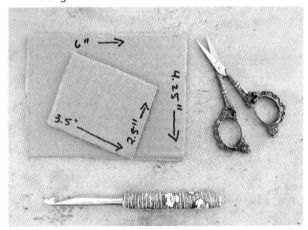

2. Loosely wrap yarn around cardboard; don't overlap.

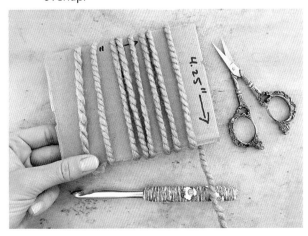

3. Use sharp scissors to cut yarn from cardboard.

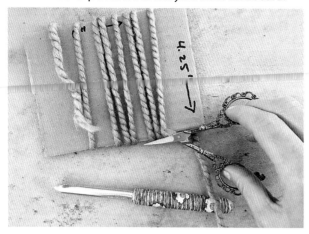

4. You'll have one piece of fringe for each yarn wrap.

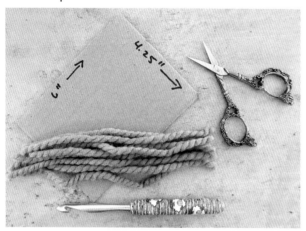

5. Fold fringe in half evenly (using desired number of yarn pieces).

6. Insert hook where fringe should be placed in crochet project and grab fringe in the middle.

7. Pull middle fold of fringe through.

8. Use hook to grab fringe yarn ends.

9. Pull yarn ends through fringe middle; pull tightly to knot.

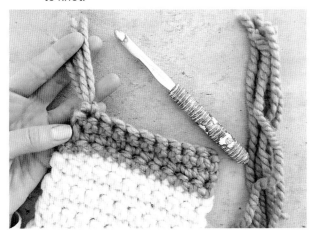

10. Repeat steps 5 through 9 for each fringe attachment.

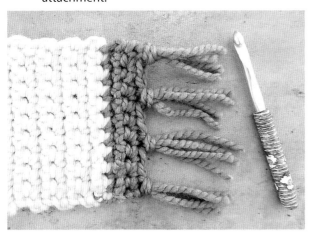

11. After all fringe is attached, trim ends to make even.

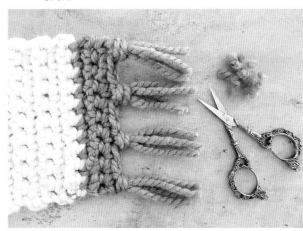

TIPS ON FRINGE

- Fringe can be added to taste, in as many (or as few) places as you want.
- Yarn can be springy, so be sure to wrap it very loosely for the most accurate lengths.
- When adding fringe, make sure all fringe knots are on the same side of your fabric.

◼ GAUGE

In crochet, gauge is in reference to measurement. Specifically, we measure gauge in terms of stitches per inch (centimeter) and rows per inch (centimeter). Most yarn labels and crochet patterns will use a 4 in. square (10 cm-square) area to determine fabric measurements (this many stitches can fit into 4 in. (10 cm) = stitch gauge, this many rows can fit into 4 in. (10 cm) = row gauge).

Stitch gauge

Row gauge

Stitch and row gauge fall into the technique section because these are directly related to fabric size, which determines project size. In short, if your project size matters (like a hat), your stitch and row gauge should match the stitch and row gauge listed in a pattern. If gauge is not crucial (like for a washcloth), your stitch and row gauge do not have to be an exact match.

As an example in gauge, each of these three swatches was worked with ten stitches and ten rows of double crochet. Without measuring, we can visibly see that each swatch is a very different size. While the three yarns used here are drastically different sizes, it is easy to see just how much the yarn and hook can alter fabric size!

Each of these swatches is 10 stitches and 10 rows of double crochet. It is easy to see that their gauge varies.

TIPS ON GAUGE

- How tightly work is held, hook size, and yarn all contribute to stitch and row gauge; altering any of these elements will alter gauge.
- If project size matters, crocheting a small swatch of the pattern will help to determine whether your gauge matches the pattern gauge.
- Remember: Matching your stitch and row gauge to a pattern is a technique that becomes easier with practice (give it time and be patient)!
- Blocking is a finishing technique applied to crochet projects that helps smooth and even out stitches, adjust and encourage shape or size, and stiffen or soften fabric. For these reasons, crochet patterns (especially in this beginner book) will not mention or require blocking. However, for a simple lesson in blocking crochet, the Ripple Wrap (see page 71) is an open stitch that will be enhanced when the fabric is wet and laid flat to dry (a type of blocking), offering gauge (size) in blocked and unblocked fabric.

LESSON 6

Stitch Patterns and First Projects—Washcloths

There are an infinite number of stitches, fabrics, and textures that you can create in crochet, and they are all combinations and variations of the basic stitches: chain, single, half double, and double crochet. Let's put it all together and make our first projects. These washcloths are a fun way to find new possibilities with just the basic stitches, and you'll have a useful item when you're finished.

TIP

Gauge and size are not crucial for these projects, so try these washcloths with any cotton yarns that you like. Cotton yarn is best for washcloths and dishcloths, but if you have trouble working with this fiber at first, try these with an acrylic yarn to get started.

SIZES/FINISHED MEASUREMENTS

One Loop Washcloth: 7 in. wide x 7.5 in. tall (17.78 cm x 19.05 cm)

Tiny Squares Washcloth: 7.25 in. wide x 7.75 in. tall (18.4 cm x 19.69 cm)

Silt Stitch Washcloth: 7.5 in. wide x 7.75 in. tall (19.05 cm x 19.69 cm)

Basic Fan Washcloth: 7.25 in. wide x 7.5 in. tall (18.4 cm x 19.69 cm)

Bobble Stitch Washcloth: 7.5 in. wide x 8 in. tall (19.05 cm x 20.32)

Waffle Stitch Washcloth: 7 in. wide x 7 in. tall (17.78 cm x 17.78 cm)

Smooth Wave Washcloth: 6.25 in. wide x 6.5 in. tall (15.88 cm x 16.51)

Bumpy Wave Washcloth: 8.5 in. wide x 7.5 in. tall (21.59 cm x 19.05)

YARN

Knit Picks CotLin DK, Light weight #3 (70% Tanguis cotton, 30% linen; 123 yd./112 m; 1.76 oz./50 g skein); 1 color (skein) per washcloth, or as many colors (skeins) as indicated in each pattern

- Swan: 1 skein
- Linen: 1 skein
- Copper: 1 skein
- Harbor: 1 skein
- Sagebrush: 1 skein

Also try: Lily Sugar 'n Cream, I Love This Cotton, Bernat Handicrafter

HOOK & OTHER MATERIALS

- US size G-6 (4.0 mm) crochet hook
- Scissors
- Yarn needle
- Measuring tape
- Stitch markers

GAUGE

Gauge is not crucial for these projects.

STITCH KEY

ch = chain
sc = single crochet
hdc = half double crochet
dc = double crochet

SPECIALTY STITCHES/TECHNIQUES

BLO = Back loop only: Work only into the back loop of a stitch.

FLO = Front loop only: Work only into the front loop of a stitch.

Fan = (2 dc, ch 1, 2 dc) worked into the same stitch.

Bobble = [Yarn over, insert hook into 1 stitch, yarn over, pull back through stitch, yarn over, pull through 2 loops on hook] 4 times total, yarn over, pull through all 5 loops on hook.

BPdc = Back post double crochet: Work a double crochet around the post of a stitch (inserting the hook from the back to the front and then to the back again), instead of into the top (front and back loops) of a stitch.

FPdc = Front post double crochet: Work a double crochet around the post of a stitch (inserting the hook from the front to the back and then to the front again), instead of into the top (front and back loops) of a stitch.

One Loop
Washcloth

This fabric is created by using just one loop (not both loops) of a stitch, which gives it a very clear texture on either side.

For project measurements, materials, and specialty stitches, refer to page 44.

■ INSTRUCTIONS

With Swan, ch 34.

Row 1: Skip 2 ch (not a st), work 1 hdc into each ch across—32 hdc.

Row 2 (right side): Ch 2 (not a st), turn, work 1 hdc into the BLO of each st across—32 hdc.

Row 3: Ch 2 (not a st), turn, work 1 hdc into the FLO of each st across—32 hdc.

Repeat Rows 2 and 3 until 20 rows complete (ending on a Row 2 repeat). Fasten off.

Sew in all ends; trim excess.

Stitch Key

⬭ Chain

┬ Half Double Crochet

⌣ Front Loop Only

⌢ Back Loop Only

One Loop Washcloth Stitch Diagram

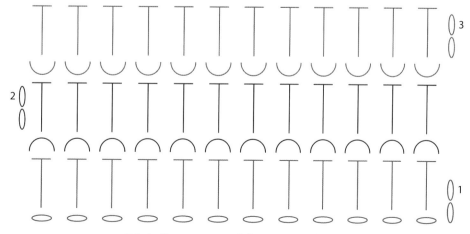

Stitch diagram not to full pattern scale.

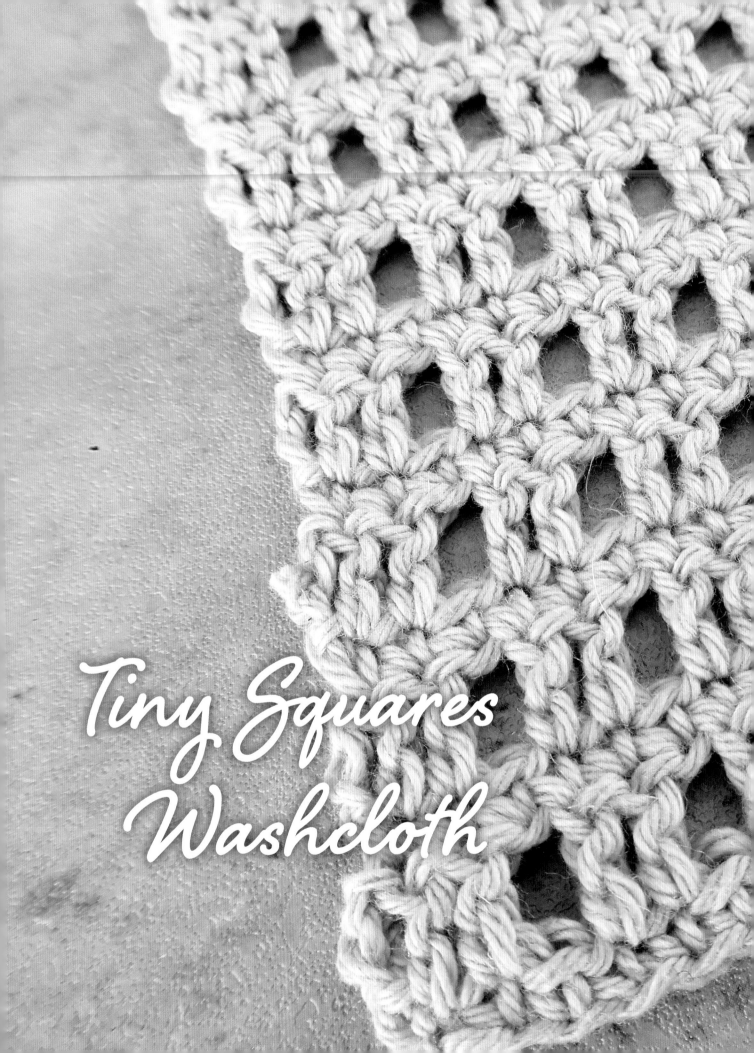

Tiny Squares Washcloth

Note the alternating pattern rows here, which give this fabric an open look.

For project measurements, materials, and specialty stitches, refer to page 44.

INSTRUCTIONS

With Linen, ch 33.

Row 1 (right side): Skip 1 ch (not a st), work 1 sc into each ch across—32 sc.

Row 2: Ch 3 (not a st), turn, work 1 dc into each of next 2 sts, [ch 1, skip 1 st, work 1 dc into each of next 2 sts] 10 times—32 sts; 22 dc + 10 ch-1 spaces.

Row 3: Ch 1 (not a st), turn, work 1 sc into each st across—32 sc.

Repeat Rows 2 and 3 until 23 rows complete (ending on a Row 3 repeat). Fasten off.

Sew in all ends; trim excess.

Stitch Key

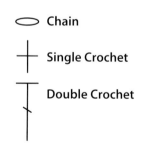

⬭ Chain

╋ Single Crochet

╤ Double Crochet

Tiny Squares Washcloth Stitch Diagram

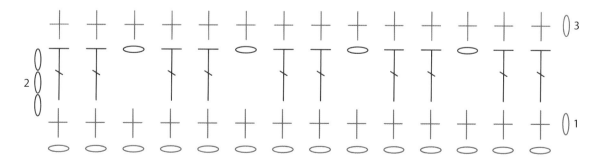

Stitch diagram not to full pattern scale.

Silt Stitch
Washcloth

This pattern has two repeating rows of stitches and a texture that is created by skipping stitches and then working multiple stitches into one space.

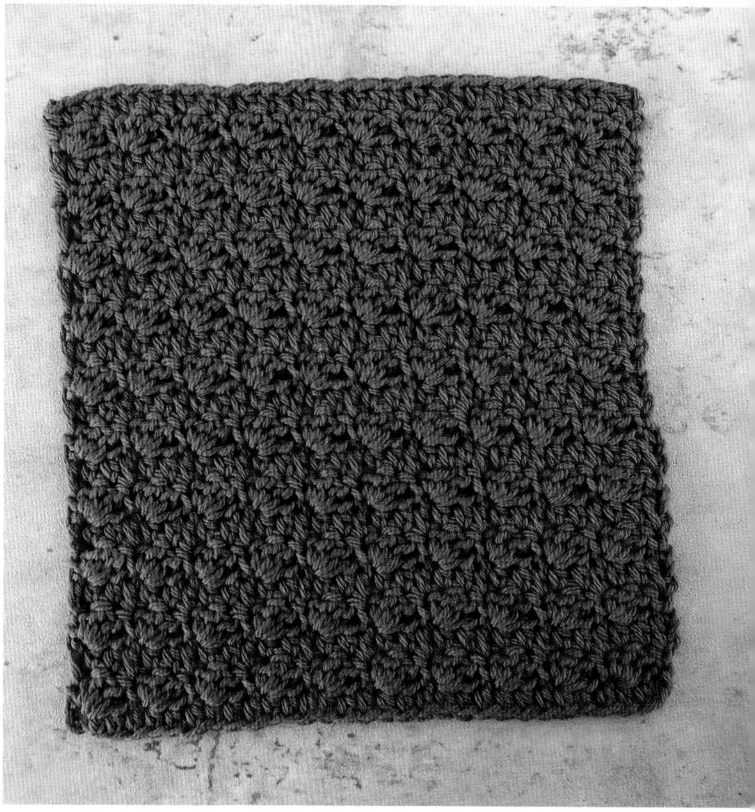

For project measurements, materials, and specialty stitches, refer to page 44.

INSTRUCTIONS

With Copper, ch 33.

Row 1 (right side): Skip 2 ch (not a st), work 1 hdc into each ch across—31 hdc.

Row 2: Ch 1 (not a st), turn, [(sc, 2 dc in same st), skip 2 sts] 10 times, sc into last st of row—31 sts; 11 sc + 20 dc.

Row 3: Ch 2 (not a st), turn, work 1 hdc into each st across—31 hdc.

Repeat Rows 2 and 3 until 21 rows complete (ending on a Row 3 repeat). Fasten off.

Sew in all ends; trim excess.

Stitch Key

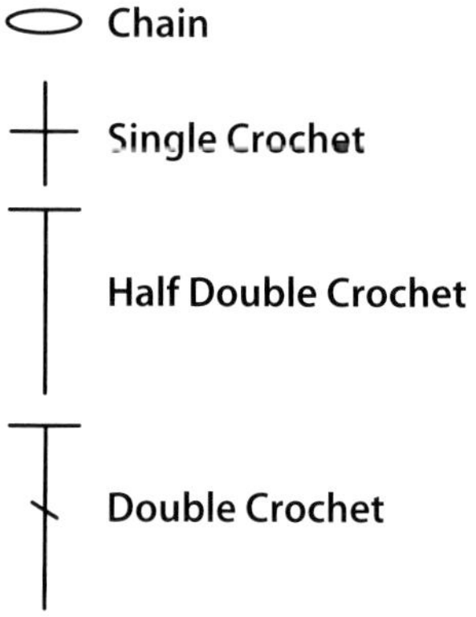
Chain
Single Crochet
Half Double Crochet
Double Crochet

Silt Stitch Washcloth Stitch Diagram

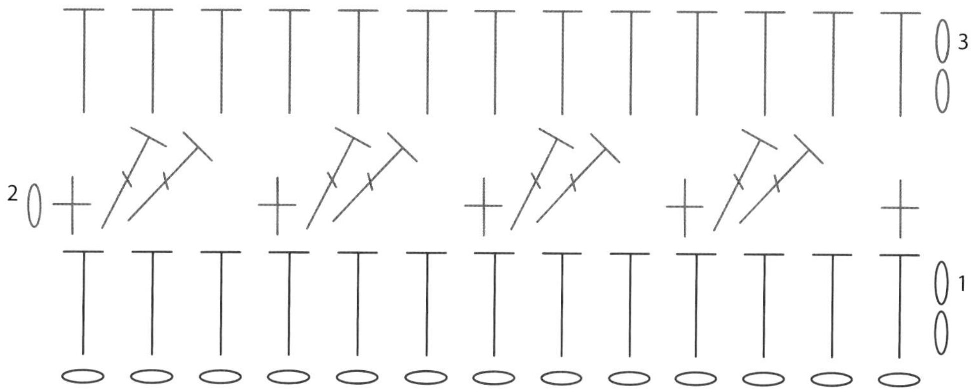
3
2
1

Stitch diagram not to full pattern scale.

Basic Fan Washcloth

This basic Fan stitch is created when multiple stitches are worked into one stitch, with skipped stitches on either side. Note the two repeating rows that make the edges straight.

For project measurements, materials, and specialty stitches, refer to page 44.

■ INSTRUCTIONS

With Harbor, ch 32.

Row 1: Skip 1 ch (not a st), [sc, skip 2 ch, Fan, skip 2 ch] 5 times, sc into last st of row—6 sc + 5 Fans.

Row 2: Ch 3 (first dc), turn, work 2 dc into same st, sc into next ch-1 space, [Fan into next sc, sc into next ch-1 space] 4 times, work 3 dc into last st of row—6 dc + 5 sc + 4 Fans.

Row 3: Ch 1 (not a st), turn, sc, [Fan into next sc, sc into next ch-1 space] 4 times, Fan into next sc, sc into last st of row—6 sc + 5 Fans.

Repeat Rows 2 and 3 until 17 rows complete (ending on a Row 3 repeat). Fasten off.

Sew in all ends, trim excess.

Stitch Key

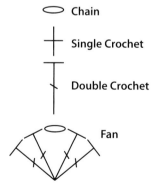

Basic Fan Washcloth Stitch Diagram

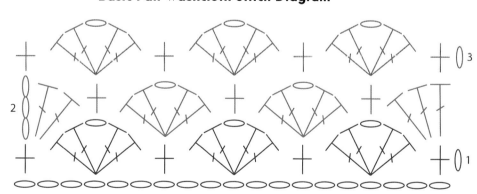

Stitch diagram not to full pattern scale.

Bobble Stitch Washcloth

The Bobble is a complex stitch that creates a lot of texture and bulk. This two-row repeat gives each side of this fabric a slightly different look.

For project measurements, materials, and specialty stitches, refer to page 44.

INSTRUCTIONS

With Sagebrush, ch 32.

Row 1: Skip 1 ch (not a st), work 1 sc into each ch across—31 sc.

Row 2 (right side): Ch 4 (first dc + ch-1 space), turn, skip 1 st, [Bobble, ch 1, skip 1 st] 14 times, dc into last st of row—2 dc + 15 ch-1 spaces + 14 Bobbles.

Row 3: Ch 1 (not a st), turn, work 1 sc into each st across—31 sc.

Repeat Rows 2 and 3 until 21 rows complete (ending on a Row 3 repeat). Fasten off.

Sew in all ends; trim excess.

Stitch Key

⌒ Chain

┼ Single Crochet

┬ Double Crochet

Bobble

Bobble Stitch Washcloth Stitch Diagram

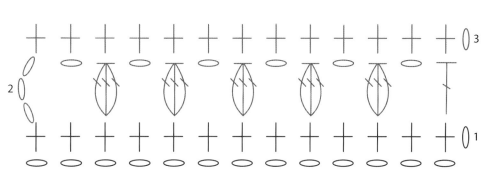

Stitch diagram not to full pattern scale.

Waffle Stitch Washcloth

This waffle-like fabric is created by working a stitch around the post of a stitch instead of through both loops of the top of it.

For project measurements, materials, and specialty stitches, refer to page 44.

▮ INSTRUCTIONS

With Swan, ch 32.

Row 1: Skip 2 ch (not a st), work 1 dc into each ch across—30 dc.

Row 2: Ch 2 (not a st), turn, [dc, FPdc] 15 times—30 sts; 15 dc + 15 FPdc.

Repeat Row 2 until 16 rows complete. Fasten off.

Sew in all ends; trim excess.

Stitch Key

⬭ Chain

╂ Double Crochet

╊ Front Post Double Crochet

Waffle Stitch Washcloth Stitch Diagram

Stitch diagram not to full pattern scale.

Smooth Wave
Washcloth

This pattern design is really notable when different colors are used. The alternating groups of single and double crochet stitches further add a very clever boxy pattern.

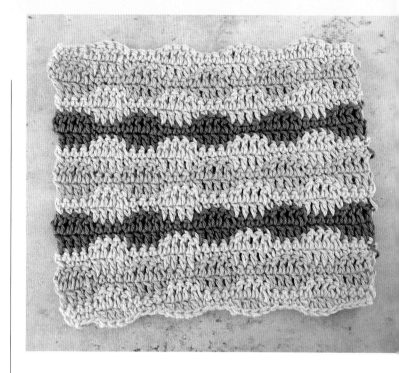

For project measurements, materials, and specialty stitches, refer to page 44.

Color Changes

Linen = Rows 1–2, 5–6, 9–10, 13–14, 17–18, 21–22
Sage = Rows 3–4, 11–12, 19–20
Harbor = Rows 7–8, 15–16
Note: Fasten off colors after each change, for rows indicated above.

■ INSTRUCTIONS

Ch 37.

Row 1: Skip 1 ch (not a st), sc into next 4 ch, [dc into next 4 ch, sc into next 4 ch] 4 times—36 sts; 20 sc + 16 dc.

Row 2: Ch 1 (not a st), turn, sc into next 4 sts, [dc into next 4 sts, sc into next 4 sts] 4 times—36 sts; 20 sc + 16 dc.

Row 3: Ch 2 (not a st), turn, dc into next 4 sts, [sc into next 4 sts, dc into next 4 sts] 4 times—36 sts; 20 dc + 16 sc.

Row 4: Ch 2 (not a st), turn, dc into next 4 sts, [sc into next 4 sts, dc into next 4 sts] 4 times—36 sts; 20 dc + 16 sc.

Row 5: Ch 1 (not a st), turn, sc into next 4 ch, [dc into next 4 ch, sc into next 4 ch] 4 times—36 sts; 20 sc + 16 dc.

Row 6: Ch 1 (not a st), turn, sc into next 4 ch, [dc into next 4 ch, sc into next 4 ch] 4 times—36 sts; 20 sc + 16 dc.

Repeat Rows 3 through 6 until 22 rows complete (ending on a Row 6 repeat). Fasten off after last row worked.

Sew in all ends; trim excess.

Stitch Key

⬭ Chain

✝ Single Crochet

╪ Double Crochet

Smooth Wave Washcloth Stitch Diagram

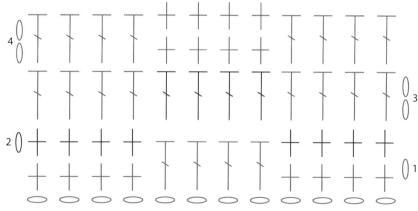

Stitch diagram not to full pattern scale.

Bumpy Wave
Washcloth

This pattern mimics the Smooth Wave Washcloth pattern, but it adds post stitches to give a bumpy look on one side. Color is also important here to make the design pop.

For project measurements, materials, and specialty stitches, refer to page 44.

INSTRUCTIONS

With Harbor, ch 29.

Row 1: Skip 1 ch (not a st), sc into next 4 ch, [dc into next 4 ch, sc into next 4 ch] 3 times—28 sts; 16 sc + 12 dc.

Row 2 (right side): Ch 1 (not a st), turn, sc into next 4 sts, [BPdc around next 4 sts, sc into next 4 sts] 3 times, fasten off Harbor—28 sts; 16 sc + 12 BPdc.

Row 3: With Linen, ch 2 (not a st), turn, dc into next 4 sts, [sc into next 4 sts, dc into next 4 sts] 3 times—28 sts; 16 dc + 12 sc.

Row 4: Ch 2 (not a st), turn, BPdc around next 4 sts, [sc into next 4 sts, BPdc into next 4 sts] 3 times, fasten off Linen—28 sts; 16 BPdc + 12 sc.

Row 5: With Harbor, ch 1 (not a st), turn, sc into next 4 sts, [dc into next 4 sts, sc into next 4 sts] 3 times—28 sts; 16 sc + 12 dc.

Row 6: Ch 1 (not a st), turn, sc into next 4 sts, [BPdc around next 4 sts, sc into next 4 sts] 3 times, fasten off Harbor—28 sts; 16 sc + 12 BPdc.

Repeat Rows 3 through 6 until 22 rows complete (ending on a Row 6 repeat). Fasten off after last row worked.

Sew in all ends; trim excess.

Stitch Key

⬭ Chain

┼ Single Crochet

╤ Double Crochet

╤ Back Post Double Crochet

Bumpy Wave Washcloth Stitch Diagram

Stitch diagram not to full pattern scale.

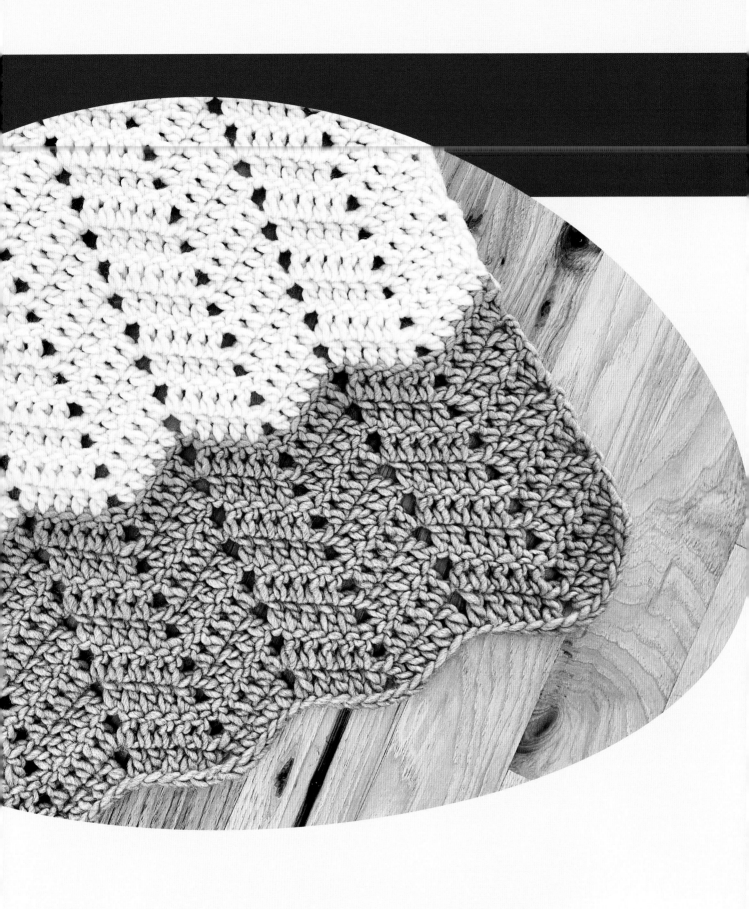

Crochet in Rows

Rows of crochet stitches can make all kinds of projects, and not just ones for beginners!

Every project in this section is worked with a combination of basic stitches, including the Fringe Wall Hanging, which teaches a new complex stitch: the Puff. Fabric gauge and project size are relaxed here, including the Linen Head Wrap—which you can measure as you go.

Fringe Table Runner

Using just chains and double crochet stitches, this table runner is a great beginner project to try.

Tip: Gauge and size are not crucial here, so you can relax and have fun while you practice your stitches.

SIZES/FINISHED MEASUREMENTS
13 in. wide x 55 in. long (33.02 cm x. 139.7 cm) (without fringe)

YARN
Lily Sugar 'n Cream, Medium weight #4 (100% cotton; 710 yd./650 m; 14 oz./400 g skein):
- Off White: 1 skein (400 yd./365.76 m for runner + 50 yd./45.72 m for fringe)

Also try: Paintbox Yarns Recycled Cotton Worsted, Peaches & Creme, Bernat Handicrafter Cotton

HOOK & OTHER MATERIALS
- US size G-6 (4.0 mm) crochet hook
- Scissors
- Yarn needle
- Measuring tape
- Stitch markers

GAUGE
16 pattern sts = 4.5 in. (11.43 cm), 9 pattern rows = 6 in. (15.24 cm)
Gauge is not crucial for this project.

STITCH KEY
ch = chain
dc = double crochet

NOTE
Length may be adjusted by adding or omitting rows, as desired. Either side of fabric can be right side (fabric is reversible).

■ INSTRUCTIONS

Ch 47.

Row 1: Skip 2 ch (not a st), work 1 dc into following 5 sts, [ch 3, skip 3 sts, work 1 dc into following 5 sts] 5 times—45 sts; 30 dc + 15 ch.

Row 2: Ch 2 (not a st), turn, work 1 dc into following 5 sts, [ch 3, skip 3 sts, work 1 dc into following 5 sts] 5 times—45 sts; 30 dc + 15 ch.

Repeat Row 2 until 81 rows complete. Fasten off.

Weave in ends; trim.

Fringe

1 Fringe Bundle = 2 strands of yarn, 12 in. (30.5 cm) each

Evenly place 1 fringe bundle into each dc st across Row 1 (30 total) and Row 81 (30 total); 60 total bundles. Trim ends evenly.

Stitch Key

⬭ Chain

╪ Double Crochet

Fringe Table Runner Stitch Diagram

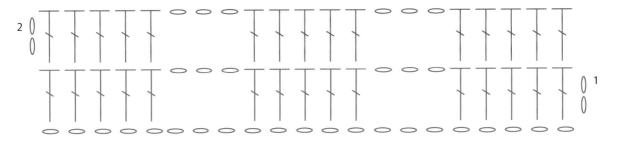

Stitch diagram not to full pattern scale.

Basic Chevron Blanket

Increasing and decreasing stitches doesn't have to be complicated, and you can make really creative patterns like this classic wave design!

Tip: The bulky yarn weight makes it easy to see each stitch, so make sure you're counting where to skip stitches and where to add them.

SIZE/FINISHED MEASUREMENTS
35 x 45 (45 x 55, 55 x 65) in./88.9 x 114.3 (114.3 x 139.7, 139.7 x 165.1) cm

NOTE

For patterns like this with more than one size, make sure you follow only the number that corresponds to the size you want to make. For example, if you want to make the 45 in. x 55 in. blanket, you will work the number of stitches just inside the first parentheses throughout the pattern. If only one number is given, it applies to all sizes. It may be helpful to highlight the numbers for your chosen size.

YARN
Bernat Roving, Bulky weight #5 (80% acrylic, 20% wool; 120 yd./109 m; 3.5 oz./100 g skein):
- Low Tide (Color A): 2 (3, 4) skeins
- Rice Paper (Color B): 4 (6, 9) skeins

Also try: Red Heart Super Saver Chunky, Bernat Symphony, Loops & Threads Waterford Big!

HOOK & OTHER MATERIALS
- US size K-10.5 (6.5 mm) crochet hook
- Scissors
- Yarn needle
- Measuring tape
- Stitch markers

GAUGE
12 pattern sts = 5 in. (12.7 cm), 6 rows = 5.5 in. (13.97 cm)

STITCH KEY
ch = chain
dc = double crochet

■ INSTRUCTIONS

35 x 45 (45 x 55, 55 x 65) in./88.9 x 114.3 (114.3 x 139.7, 139.7 x 165.1) cm

With Color A, ch 87 (111, 135).

Row 1: Skip 3 ch (first dc), dc, dc into next 4 ch, [skip 2 ch, dc into next 5 ch, ch 2, dc into next 5 ch], until 7 ch remain, skip 2 ch, dc into next 4 ch, work 2 dc into last ch—84 (108, 132) sts; 72 (92, 112) dc + 6 (8, 10) ch-2 spaces.

Row 2: Ch 3 (first dc), turn, dc into same st, dc into next 4 sts, [skip 2 sts, dc into next 5 sts, ch 2, dc into next 5 sts] until 7 sts remain, skip 2 sts, dc into next 4 sts, work 2 dc into last st—84 (108, 132) sts; 72 (92, 112) dc + 6 (8, 10) ch-2 spaces.

Repeat Row 2 for each size as follows:

35 in. x 45 in. (88.9 cm x 114.3 cm): Color A = Rows 1–8, Color B = Rows 9–37, Color A = Rows 38–45

45 in. x 55 in. (114.3 cm x 139.7 cm): Color A = Rows 1–9, Color B = Rows 10–46, Color A = Rows 47–55

55 in. x 65 in. (139.7 cm x 165.1 cm): Color A = Rows 1–10, Color B = Rows 11–55, Color A = Rows 56–65

Fasten off after last row worked. Sew in ends; trim excess.

Stitch Key

⬯ Chain

╪ Double Crochet

Basic Chevron Blanket Stitch Diagram

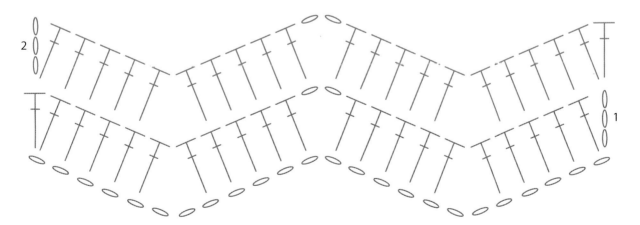

Stitch diagram not to full pattern scale.

Ripple Wrap

Worked back and forth in rows, this wrap grows in length with each new row added. Simple chain, single, and double crochet stitches are used to create this open fabric, with a short repeat for the stitches and just two repeating rows.

Tip: Try this project with other weights, types, and colors of yarn!

SIZE/FINISHED MEASUREMENTS
One size
Unblocked fabric: 21 in. wide x 72 in. long (53.34 cm. x 182.88 cm) (without fringe)
Blocked fabric: 22 in. wide x 82 in. long (55.88 cm x 208.28 cm) (without fringe)

YARN
Caron Cotton Ripple Cakes, Light weight #3 (100% cotton; 491 yd./449 m; 8.5 oz./240 g cake):
- Iced Latte: 2 cakes

Also try: Cascade Yarns Fixation, Red Heart Yarns Unforgettable, Lion Brand Yarn Shawl in a Ball

HOOK & OTHER MATERIALS
- US size G-8 (4.0 mm) crochet hook
- Scissors
- Yarn needle
- Measuring tape
- Stitch markers

GAUGE
Unblocked fabric: 21.5 sts = 4 in. (10.16 cm), 10 rows = 5.3 in. (13.46 cm)
Blocked fabric: 20.5 pattern sts = 4 in. (10.16 cm), 10 pattern rows = 6 in. (13.46 cm)

STITCH KEY
ch = chain
sc = single crochet
dc = double crochet

NOTE

Open fabrics like this one tend to not take shape, so wetting the fabric and carefully laying it flat to dry may help to set the stitches, resulting in a more even-looking fabric. You can see the difference this step makes in the gauge section with the blocked versus unblocked fabric dimensions.

INSTRUCTIONS

Ch 114.
Row 1: Skip 1 ch (not a st), sc, [ch 1, skip 3 ch, (dc, ch 4, dc) into next st, ch 1, skip 3 ch, sc] 14 times—127 sts; 28 dc + 15 sc + 84 ch.
Row 2: Ch 3 (first dc), turn, dc into same st, [ch 1, sc into next ch-4 space, ch 1, (dc, ch 4, dc) into next sc] 13 times, ch 1, sc into next ch-4 space, ch 1, work 2 dc into last sc—124 sts; 30 dc + 80 ch + 14 sc.
Row 3: Ch 1 (not a st), turn, sc, [ch 1, (dc, ch 4, dc) into next sc, ch 1, sc into next ch-4 space] 13 times, ch 1, (dc, ch 4, dc) into next sc, ch 1, sc into last st—127 sts; 28 dc + 15 sc + 84 ch.

Repeat Rows 2 and 3 until 135 rows complete (ending on a Row 3 repeat). Fasten off.
Weave in ends; trim excess.

Fringe
1 Fringe Bundle = 5 strands of yarn, 14 in. (35.56 cm) each.

Evenly place 1 fringe bundle into each ch-4 space across Row 135 and ch-4 space across Row 2 (over and through Row 1).
Trim ends evenly.

Stitch Key

⊙ Chain

✛ Single Crochet

┬ Double Crochet

Ripple Wrap Stitch Diagram

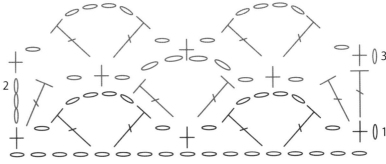

Stitch diagram not to full pattern scale.

Linen Head Wrap

This pattern is worked by length, so you can easily measure the fabric or try it on for size as you work each row.

Tip: You can try alternate yarn weights with this pattern as long as you pay close attention to the finished length of your head wrap.

SIZES/FINISHED MEASUREMENTS
4 in. wide x 16 (18, 20, 22, 24) in. long (10.16 cm wide x 40.64, 45.72, 50.8, 55.88, 60.96 cm long)

YARN
Lion Brand Yarn Wool Ease, Medium weight #4 (80% acrylic, 20% wool; 197 yd./180 m; 3 oz./85 g skein):
- Linen: 1 skein

Also try: Hayfield Bonus Aran with Wool, Stylecraft Special Aran with Wool, King Cole Acorn Aran

HOOK & OTHER MATERIALS
- US size I-9 (5.5 mm) crochet hook
- Scissors
- Yarn needle
- Measuring tape
- Stitch markers

GAUGE
25 pattern sts = 4 in. (10.16 cm), 7 pattern rows = 4 in. (10.16 cm)

STITCH KEY
ch = chain
sc = single crochet
dc = double crochet

NOTES
- For the best fit, measure around at forehead and follow pattern size that is the closest match.
- Either side of fabric can be right side (it's reversible).

■ INSTRUCTIONS

Leave a 12 in. (30.48 cm) tail, ch 18.
Row 1: Skip 1 ch (not a st), [(sc, ch 2, 3 dc) into same st, skip 3 sts] 4 times, sc—25 sts; 5 sc + 12 dc + 8 ch.
Row 2: Ch 1 (not a st), turn, (sc, ch 2, 3 dc) into same st, [(sc, ch 2, 3 dc) into ch-2 space] 3 times, sc into last ch-2 space of row—25 sts; 5 sc + 12 dc + 8 ch.
Repeat Row 2 until 28 (31, 34, 37, 40) rows complete, leave a 12 in. (30.48 cm) tail. Fasten off.

Finishing
Thread yarn needle with 12 in. (30.48 cm) tail from Row 1.
Hold Row 1 with last row completed; sew both thicknesses together just 4 times (1 in./2.54 cm gaps between each stitch).
Pull tail end to cinch fabric; tie beginning and ending tail ends together to fasten.
Sew in ends; trim excess.

Stitch Key
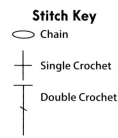
⬯ Chain
┼ Single Crochet
│ Double Crochet

Linen Head Wrap Stitch Diagram

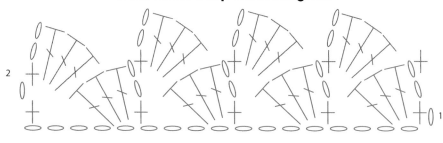

Fringe Wall Hanging

Worked from the bottom point up toward the twig, this wall hanging is worked back and forth in rows and evenly increases until Row 16. This piece uses chains and double crochet stitches and includes alternating rows of puffs for simple texture.

Tip: Gauge and size are not crucial, so have fun with any yarn weight/fiber/type and color with this project to create your own unique piece of wall art!

SIZE/FINISHED MEASUREMENTS
16 in. wide x 24 in. long (40.64 cm x 60.96 cm) (from center point, without fringe)

YARN
Lion Brand Yarn 24/7 Cotton, Medium weight #4 (100% mercerized cotton; 186 yd./170 m; 3.5 oz./100 g skein):
- Camel: 2 skeins

Also try: Loops & Threads Cotton Colors, Peaches & Creme, Hobbii Rainbow Cotton 8/8

HOOK & OTHER MATERIALS
- US size G-6 (4.0 mm) crochet hook
- Scissors
- Yarn needle
- Measuring tape
- Stitch markers
- 20 in. (50.8 cm) twig or dowel

GAUGE
16.25 pattern sts = 4 in. (10.16 cm), 7 pattern rows = 4 in. (10.16 cm)

STITCH KEY
ch = chain
sc = single crochet
dc = double crochet

SPECIALTY STITCH
Puff: [Yarn over, insert hook into st, yarn over, pull through st] 3 times, yarn over, pull through all 7 loops on hook.

NOTE
Any yarn weight/type may be used, as desired; gauge and size are not crucial for this project.

■ INSTRUCTIONS

Row 1 (right side): Ch 5 (first dc + ch 1 + base ch), (dc, ch 1, dc) into fifth ch from hook—5 sts; 3 dc + 2 ch.

Row 2: Ch 4 (first dc + ch-1 space, here and throughout), turn, dc into same st, ch 1, skip 1 st, Puff, ch 1, skip 1 st, (dc, ch 1, dc) into last st of row—9 sts; 4 dc + 4 ch + 1 Puff.

Row 3: Ch 4, turn, dc into same st, [ch 1, skip 1 st, dc] until 2 sts remain, ch 1, skip 1 st, (dc, ch 1, dc) into last st of row—13 sts; 7 dc + 6 ch.

Row 4: Ch 4, turn, dc into same st, [ch 1, skip 1 st, Puff] until 2 sts remain, ch 1, skip 1 st, (dc, ch 1, dc) into last st of row—17 sts; 4 dc + 8 ch + 5 Puff.

Row 5: Ch 4, turn, dc into same st, [ch 1, skip 1 st, dc] until 2 sts remain, ch 1, skip 1 st, (dc, ch 1, dc) into last st of row—21 sts: 11 dc + 10 ch.

Row 6: Ch 4, turn, dc into same st, [ch 1, skip 1 st, Puff] until 2 sts remain, ch 1, skip 1 st, (dc, ch 1, dc) into last st of row—25 sts; 4 dc + 12 ch + 9 Puff.

Row 7: Ch 4, turn, dc into same st, [ch 1, skip 1 st, dc] until 2 sts remain, ch 1, skip 1 st, (dc, ch 1, dc) into last st of row—29 sts; 15 dc + 14 ch.

Row 8: Ch 4, turn, dc into same st, [ch 1, skip 1 st, Puff] until 2 sts remain, ch 1, skip 1 st, (dc, ch 1, dc) into last st of row—33 sts; 4 dc + 16 ch + 13 Puff.

Row 9: Ch 4, turn, dc into same st, [ch 1, skip 1 st, dc] until 2 sts remain, ch 1, skip 1 st, (dc, ch 1, dc) into last st of row—37 sts; 19 dc + 18 ch.

Row 10: Ch 4, turn, dc into same st, [ch 1, skip 1 st, Puff] until 2 sts remain, ch 1, skip 1 st, (dc, ch 1, dc) into last st of row—41 sts; 4 dc + 20 ch + 17 Puff.

Row 11: Ch 4, turn, dc into same st, [ch 1, skip 1 st, dc] until 2 sts remain, ch 1, skip 1 st, (dc, ch 1, dc) into last st of row—45 sts; 23 dc + 22 ch.

Row 12: Ch 4, turn, dc into same st, [ch 1, skip 1 st, Puff] until 2 sts remain, ch 1, skip 1 st, (dc, ch 1, dc) into last st of row—49 sts; 4 dc + 24 ch + 21 Puff.

Row 13: Ch 4, turn, dc into same st, [ch 1, skip 1 st, dc] until 2 sts remain, ch 1, skip 1 st, (dc, ch 1, dc) into last st of row—53 sts; 27 dc + 26 ch.

Row 14: Ch 4, turn, dc into same st, [ch 1, skip 1 st, Puff] until 2 sts remain, ch 1, skip 1 st, (dc, ch 1, dc) into last st of row—57 sts; 4 dc + 28 ch + 25 Puff.

Row 15: Ch 4, turn, dc into same st, [ch 1, skip 1 st, dc] until 2 sts remain, ch 1, skip 1 st, (dc, ch 1, dc) into last st of row—61 sts; 31 dc + 30 ch.

Stitch Key

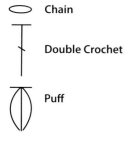

Chain

Double Crochet

Puff

Fringe Wall Hanging Stitch Diagram

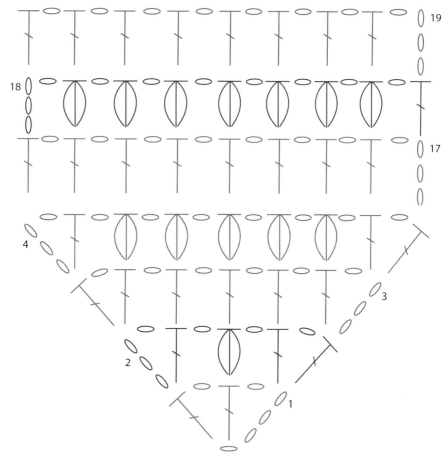

Stitch diagram not to full pattern scale.

Row 16: Ch 4, turn, dc into same st, [ch 1, skip 1 st, Puff] until 2 sts remain, ch 1, skip 1 st, (dc, ch 1, dc) into last st of row—65 sts; 4 dc + 32 ch + 29 Puff.

Row 17: Ch 4, turn, skip 1 st, dc, [ch 1, skip 1 st, dc] across row—65 sts; 33 dc + 32 ch.

Row 18: Ch 4, turn, skip 1 st, Puff, [ch 1, skip 1 st, Puff] until 2 sts remain, ch 1, skip 1 st, dc into last st of row—65 sts; 2 dc + 32 ch + 31 Puff.

Repeat Rows 17 and 18 until 45 rows complete (ending on a Row 17 repeat).

Row 46: Ch 100 (hanger), turn, skip 64 sts, sc into last st of row; fasten off—101 sts; 100 ch + 1 sc.

Fringe

Fringe bundle = Cut 5 strands of yarn measuring 14 in. (35.56 cm) each, fold in half evenly, loop ends around a stitch space and pull back through center to knot.

Create 1 fringe bundle and attach around center dc in Row 1, and to each side of the following end Rows: 3, 5, 7, 9, 11, 13, 15, 17.

Finishing

Evenly weave twig/dowel between dc sts across Row 45. Weave in all ends; trim excess.

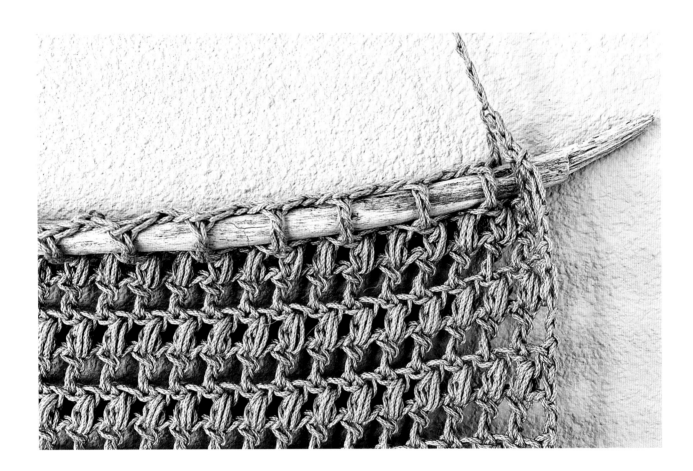

Crochet in Tubes

Tubes are just rows of crochet that connect in some way, either with a joining technique or in continuous rounds. If you can crochet in rows, you can crochet in tubes too! When working rows of crochet, you'll turn at the end of each row to begin a new row of work. But here you'll be working in rows that connect to form tubes. There are two ways you can work in tubes: joined and continuous rounds.

TUBES IN JOINED ROUNDS

Joined rounds use slip stitches as the joining technique, and they are worked after all stitches are followed in a pattern round. However, you only use the slip stitch here as a joining technique, so the slip stitch does not count as a stitch (even though you can see them, which cause a noticeable seam).

top of first stitch (st marker)

ch 3 (first st)

sl st (not a st)

Double crochet tube with joined rounds.

TUTORIAL: TUBES IN JOINED ROUNDS

Joined Double Crochet Tube Stitch Pattern

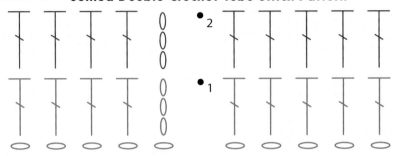

Stitch diagram not to full pattern scale.

1. Chain 15.

2. Insert hook into first chain formed.

3. Yarn over hook.

Stitch Key

⬭ Chain

● Slip Stitch

T Double Crochet

4. Pull yarn through chain and loop on hook (slip stitch).

5. Chain 3 (first double crochet); place stitch marker.

11

1

6. Find next stitch.

7. Work 1 double crochet into each stitch around (15 total).

8. Insert hook into top of first double crochet.

9. Yarn over hook.

10. Pull yarn through stitch and loop on hook (slip stitch).

11. Round 2: Chain 3 (first double crochet); place stitch marker.

12. Repeat steps 6 through 10. Round 2 complete.

Now try a few patterns that are worked in joined rounds on the following pages!

Infinity Scarf

This infinity scarf is worked in a tube and joined after each round with a slip stitch. This is an easy project to get familiar with working in joined rounds.

Tip: Make this infinity scarf as long or short as you like by adding or omitting rounds of crochet. You can easily try this scarf on as you go to get the right length.

SIZE/FINISHED MEASUREMENTS
One size: 5 in. (12.7 cm) flat (10 in./25.4 cm around) x 72 in. (182.88 cm) long

YARN
Lion Brand Yarn Mandala Watercolors, Bulky weight #5 (75% acrylic, 15% wool, 10% nylon; 164 yd./150 m; 3.5 oz./100 g cake):
- Almond: 3 cakes

Also try: Red Heart Soft Essentials, Bernat Wavelength, Lion Brand Yarn Scarfie

HOOK & OTHER MATERIALS
- US size K-10.5 (6.5 mm) crochet hook
- Scissors
- Yarn needle
- Measuring tape
- Stitch markers

GAUGE
19.5 pattern sts = 5 in. (12.7 cm), 4 pattern rows = 3 in. (7.62 cm)

STITCH KEY
ch = chain
dc = double crochet
sl st = slip stitch

▮▮ INSTRUCTIONS

Ch 39, sl st into first ch to join.

Round 1 (right side): Ch 4 (first dc + ch-1 space), dc into same ch, skip 2 ch, [(dc, ch 1, dc) into next st, skip 2 ch] 12 times, sl st into beginning ch-1 space to join—39 sts; 26 dc + 13 ch-1 spaces.

Round 2: Ch 4 (first dc + ch-1 space), dc into same space, (dc, ch 1, dc) into each ch-1 space around, sl st into beginning ch-1 space to join—39 sts; 26 dc + 13 ch-1 spaces.

Repeat Round 2 until 95 rounds are complete. Fasten off a 30 in. (76.2 cm) tail end.

Stitch Key

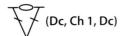

⌒ Chain

⟨Y⟩ (Dc, Ch 1, Dc)

● Slip Stitch

Infinity Scarf Stitch Diagram

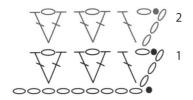

2

1

Stitch diagram not to full pattern scale.

Finishing

Ensure right side of tube is facing outward.

Align sl st seam into a straight line along one side (don't twist the seam/fabric).

With 30 in. (76.2 cm) tail end, evenly sew Round 95 to Round 1.

Sew in all ends, trim excess.

Landscapes Cowl

As with the Infinity Scarf, this cowl is worked in joined rounds to form a tube. In addition to using the slip stitch here as a joining technique for each round of work, you'll use it to create fabric on Rounds 2 and 3. This project uses three different rounds of stitch patterns, so pay careful attention to those repeats.

Tip: Keeping within the medium-weight yarn category (4), use a yarn that you think is most comfortable around your neck and close to your skin (whatever that fiber content may be).

SIZE/FINISHED MEASUREMENTS
28 in. (71.12 cm) around (14 in./35.56 cm flat) x 8.5 in. (21.59 cm) tall

YARN
Lion Brand Yarn Landscapes, Medium weight #4 (100% acrylic; 147 yd./134 m; per 3.5 oz./100 g skein):
- Sage: 2 skeins

Also try: Lion Brand Yarn Heartland, Red Heart Soft, Lion Brand Yarn Landscapes Fusion

HOOK & OTHER MATERIALS
- US size K-10.5 (6.5 mm) crochet hook
- Scissors
- Yarn needle
- Measuring tape
- Stitch markers

GAUGE
12 pattern sts = 4 in. (10.16 cm), 8 pattern rows = 3 in. (7.62 cm)

STITCH KEY
ch = chain
sc = single crochet
dc = double crochet
sl st = slip stitch

SPECIALTY STITCH/TECHNIQUE
BLO = Work into the back loop only.

■ INSTRUCTIONS

Ch 84, sl st into first ch to join.

Round 1 (right side): Ch 1 (not a st), sc into each ch around, sl st into top of first st to join—84 sc.

Rounds 2–3: Ch 1 (not a st), sl st into BLO of each st around, sl st into top of first st to join—84 sl st.

Round 4: Ch 3 (first dc), dc into same st, work 2 dc into each st around, sl st into top of first st to join—168 dc.

Round 5: Ch 1 (not a st), [sc, skip 1 st] 84 times, sl st into top of first st to join—84 sc.

Repeat Rounds 2 through 5 until 23 rounds complete (ending on a Round 3 repeat). Fasten off after last round worked.

Sew in ends; trim excess.

Landscapes Cowl Stitch Diagram

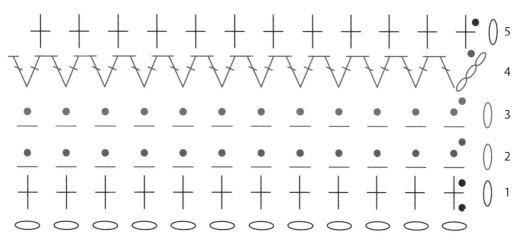

Stitch diagram not to full pattern scale.

Stitch Key

⬭ Chain

● Slip Stitch

+ Single Crochet

•⎯ Slip Stitch (Back Loop Only)

V 2 Double Crochet into 1 Stitch

Ecru Backpack

This backpack is worked in joined rounds of crochet from the bottom up. However, the bottom end is joined together to close with a row of slip stitches (yet another use for the slip stitch that's fun to try!). This pattern is worked with chains, single crochet, and double crochet stitches over four repeating rounds of work, creating the open fabric.

Tip: Choose a sturdy yarn for this backpack to create a functional project. While cotton was used here, synthetic fibers may be okay too.

SIZE/FINISHED MEASUREMENTS
25 in. (63.5 cm) wide (12.5 in./31.75 cm flat) x 13.5 in. (34.29 cm) long (excluding drawstring straps)

YARN
Lion Brand Yarn 24/7 Cotton, Medium weight #4 (100% mercerized cotton; 186 yd./170 m; 3.5 oz./100 g skein):
- Ecru: 2 skeins

Also try: Peaches & Creme, Paintbox Yarns Recycled Cotton Worsted, Lily Sugar 'n Cream

HOOK & OTHER MATERIALS
- US size G-6 (4.0 mm) crochet hook
- Scissors
- Yarn needle
- Measuring tape
- Stitch markers

GAUGE
16 pattern sts = 4 in. (10.16 cm), 12 pattern rows = 2.5 in. (6.35 cm)

STITCH KEY
ch = chain
sl st = slip stitch
sc = single crochet
dc = double crochet

NOTES
- Backpack is worked in a tube from the bottom up in joined rounds.
- Drawstring straps are customizable, based on personal measurements.

INSTRUCTIONS

Ch 100, sl st to first ch to join.

Round 1 (right side): Ch 1 (not a st, here and throughout), work 1 sc into each ch around, sl st into top of first sc to join—100 sc.

Round 2: Ch 1, work 1 sc into each st around, sl st into top of first sc to join—100 sc.

Repeat Round 2 until 12 rounds complete.

Round 13: Ch 1, sc into next 3 sts, ch 2, skip 2 sts, dc, ch 2, skip 2 sts, [sc into next 5 sts, ch 2, skip 2 sts, dc, ch 2, skip 2 sts] around until 2 sts remain, sc into last 2 sts, sl st into top of first sc to join—100 sts; 50 sc + 20 ch-2 spaces + 10 dc.

Round 14: Ch 1, work 1 sc into each st around, sl st into top of first sc to join—100 sc.

Round 15: Ch 5 (first dc + ch-2 space), skip 2 sts, sc into next 5 sts, [ch 2, skip 2 sts, dc, ch 2, skip 2 sts, sc into next 5 sts] around until 2 sts remain, ch 2, skip 2 sts, sl st into top of first dc to join—100 sts; 50 sc + 20 ch-2 spaces + 10 dc.

Round 16: Ch 1, work 1 sc into each st around, sl st into top of first sc to join—100 sc.

Repeat Rounds 13 through 16 until 56 rounds complete (ending on a Round 16 repeat). Fasten off.

Lay Backpack flat, with right side of fabric turned inside (back of fabric turned outside). Sl st both thicknesses of Round 1 together. Knot and sew down ends to secure; trim excess. Turn back of fabric inside (right side of fabric turned outside).

Weave in all ends; trim excess.

Drawstring Straps

In a standing position, measure along the side of body from top of shoulder to midhip. Multiply measurement by 3 (drawstring measurement).

Cut six strands of yarn, each the length of your drawstring measurement (Drawstring Strap).

Lay Backpack flat.

With Round 55 as a guide, feed one end of Drawstring Strap around 9 dc sts from Round 55 (leaving 1 dc st open); Drawstring Straps face back of Backpack.

For each Drawstring Strap: Separate strands into two groups of three strands. With Round 2 as a guide, start in one corner and pull three strands through both thicknesses of fabric from back to front of Backpack, skip 2 sts, pull three strands through both thicknesses of fabric from back to front of Backpack. Ensure strands are even, loop and knot together 2 in. (5.08 cm) from end.

Stitch Key

⬯ Chain

● Slip Stitch

✛ Single Crochet

🐧 Double Crochet

Ecru Backpack Stitch Diagram

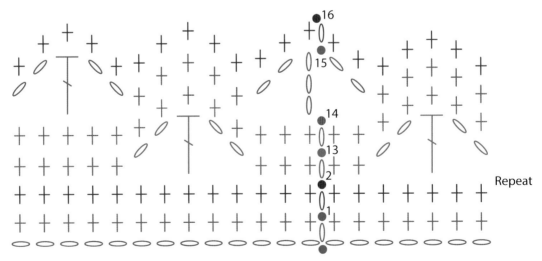

Stitch diagram not to full pattern scale.

TUBES IN CONTINUOUS ROUNDS

Tubes worked in continuous rounds begin like a row of crochet, but the first stitch of each new round is worked on top of the first stitch in the last round. This approach allows you to work in a spiral, so you won't join each new round with a slip stitch and there isn't a seam!

first stitch: round 1

last stitch: round 1

Single crochet tube with continuous rounds.

TUTORIAL: TUBES IN CONTINUOUS ROUNDS

Single Crochet Continuous Round Stitch Diagram

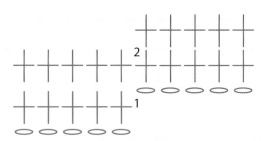

Stitch diagram not to full pattern scale.

Stitch Key

⬭ Chain

╋ Single Crochet

1. Chain 15.

2. Insert hook into first chain formed.

3. Single crochet; place stitch marker.

4. Round 1 complete.

5. Round 2: Single crochet into top of first stitch; place stitch marker.

6. Round 2 complete.

Now try a few patterns that are worked in continuous rounds on the following pages!

BLO Cup Sleeve

You'll get this texture by working single crochet stitches in the back loop only, leaving the front loop exposed. This tube is worked in a continuous circle, so it's a quick and easy project to try out the new technique.

Tip: While the yarn weight for this should be in the medium weight (#4) range, the fiber content can be synthetic or plant based if you prefer.

SIZE/FINISHED MEASUREMENTS
4.5 in. (11.43 cm) flat (9 in./22.86 cm around) x 3 in. (7.62 cm) tall

YARN
Patons Classic Wool Worsted, Medium weight #4 (100% pure new wool; 210 yd./192 m; 3.5 oz./100 g skein):
- Rich Teal: 1 skein (approx. 30 yd./27.53 m used in sample)

Also try: Knit Picks Brava Worsted, Peaches and Creme, Patons Canadiana

HOOK & OTHER MATERIALS
- US size H-8 (5.0 mm) crochet hook
- Scissors
- Yarn needle
- Measuring tape
- Stitch markers

GAUGE
16 sts = 4 in. (10.16 cm), 12 rows = 3 in. (7.62 cm)

STITCH KEY
ch = chain
sc = single crochet

SPECIALTY STITCHES/TECHNIQUES
BLO = back loop only

NOTES
- Rounds are not joined; work each in a continuous circle.
- When working continuous rounds, place one stitch marker into the top of the first stitch in each round to mark progress.

◼ INSTRUCTIONS

Leave a 10 in. (25.4 cm) tail, ch 36.

Round 1 (right side): Sc into BLO of each ch around—36 sc.

Round 2: Sc into BLO of each st around—36 sc.

Repeat Round 2 until 12 rounds are complete.

After last round worked, fasten off a 10 in. (25.4 cm) tail.

Turn Cup Sleeve so that ride side of fabric is on the inside.

Sew in both yarn ends; trim excess.

Turn Cup Sleeve so that right side of fabric is on the outside.

BLO Cup Sleeve Stitch Diagram

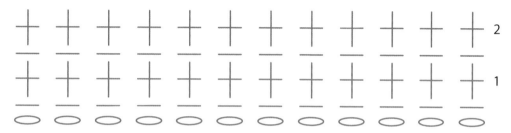

Stitch diagram not to full pattern scale.

Stitch Key

◯ Chain

┼ Single Crochet, Back Loop Only

Linen Stitch
Pillow Cover

As with the BLO Cup Sleeve, this pillow cover is worked in a continuous circle to form a tube. The stitch pattern uses chains and single crochet stitches, so it's easy to memorize, and the three blocks of colors help you to practice color changes while adding a bit of flair.

Tip: You don't have to use three solid colors here. This is a great project for trying different yarn fibers and other fun colors!

SIZES/FINISHED MEASUREMENTS
12 x 12 (16 x 16, 20 x 20) in./30.48 x 30.48 (40.64 x 40.64, 50.80 x 50.80) cm

YARN
Knit Picks Dishie, Medium weight #4 (100% cotton; 190 yd./173 m; 3.5 oz./100 g skein):
- Kenai (Color A): 1 (2, 2) skeins
- Linen (Color B): 1 (2, 2) skeins
- Swan (Color C): 1 (2, 2) skeins

Also try: Lion Brand Yarn Pima Cotton, Premier Yarns Just Cotton, Women's Institute Home Cotton

HOOK & OTHER MATERIALS
- US size G-6 (4.0 mm) crochet hook
- 12 in. (16 in., 20 in.) (30.48 cm, 40.64 cm, 50.80 cm) square pillow form
- Scissors
- Yarn needle
- Measuring tape
- Stitch markers

GAUGE
21 sts = 5 in. (12.7 cm), 18 rows = 4 in. (10.16 cm)

STITCH KEY
ch = chain
sc = single crochet

NOTES
- Rounds are not joined; work each in a continuous circle.
- When working continuous rounds, place one stitch marker into the top of the first stitch in each round to mark progress.

■ INSTRUCTIONS

12 (16, 20) in. square/30.48 (40.64, 50.8) cm. square

With Color A, leave a 40 in. (101.60 cm) tail, ch 101 (133, 165).

Round 1 (right side): Sc into first ch formed. [ch 1, skip 1 ch, sc into next ch] around—101 (133, 165) sts; 51 (67, 83) sc + 50 (66, 82) ch.

Round 2: [Ch 1, skip 1 st, sc into next ch-1 space] around—101 (133, 165) sts; 51 (67, 83) ch + 50 (66, 82) sc.

Repeat Round 2 for each size as follows:

12 in. x 12 in. (30.48 cm x 30.48 cm): Color A = 1–18, Color B = 19–36, Color C = 37–54

16 in. x 16 in. (40.64 cm x 40.64 cm): Color A = 1–24, Color B = 25–48, Color C = 49–72

20 in. x 20 in. (50.80 cm x 50.80 cm): Color A = 1–30, Color B = 31–60, Color C = 61–90

Finishing

After last round worked, fasten off a 40 in. (101.60 cm) tail.

Ensure right side of pillow is facing outward.

Use tail from Round 1 to sew both thicknesses of Round 1 together evenly.

Insert pillow form.

Use tail from last round worked to sew both thicknesses of that round together evenly.

Tassels

1 Tassel Bundle = With Color B: 10 strands of yarn, 14 in. (35.56 cm) each.

For each pillow corner, evenly knot a 20 in. (50.80 cm) strand of Color B into place, and then:

- Place 1 Tassel Bundle evenly between 20 in. (50.80 cm) strands of yarn. Use 20 in. (50.80 cm) strands to tie Tassel Bundle evenly into place.
- Fold Tassel Bundle in half, so that all strands are even. Form a loop with Tassel Bundle and pull ends through loop to create a knot. Push knot close until it is flush with pillow.

Linen Stitch Pillow Cover Stitch Diagram

Stitch Key

Stitch diagram not to full pattern scale.

LESSON 9

Crochet Increasing Rounds

Increasing rounds use simple repeats to expand the size of every new round of stitches, working from a center starting point outward!

If you can crochet tubes, you can work increasing rounds! Patterns here begin in a central point and grow with every new round by increasing the number of stitches applied. Whether you're joining each round or working in a continuous round, the stitches will continue to increase until the desired fabric size is reached. Projects like these can be a bit tricky to work at first because it is important to identify every stitch individually to ensure that flat, even fabric is being created.

INCREASING JOINED ROUNDS

The most basic way to work an increasing round is to crochet a circle. Depending on the height of the stitch within a pattern (single, half double, double), the number of stitches used to begin the round, and increase for every round after, will differ.

Increasing joined rounds in double crochet, Round 1.

Increasing joined rounds in double crochet, Round 2.

TUTORIAL: INCREASING JOINED ROUNDS

Increasing Joined Rounds in Double Crochet Stitch Diagram

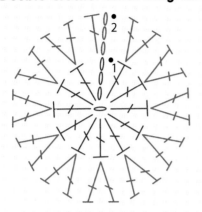

Stitch Key

⬭ Chain

• Slip Stitch

⊤ Double Crochet

⋎ 2 Double Crochet into 1 Stitch

1. Chain 4 (first double crochet + base chain).

2. Place stitch marker into both loops of last chain formed.

3. Work 11 double crochet into 4th chain from hook (12 total).

4. Insert hook into top of first double crochet.

5. Yarn over hook.

6. Pull yarn through stitch and loop on hook (slip stitch). Round 1 complete.

7. Chain 3 (first double crochet).

8. Place stitch marker into both loops of last chain formed.

9. Double crochet into same stitch.

10. Work 2 double crochet into each stitch around (24 total).

11. Insert hook into top of first double crochet.

12. Yarn over hook.

13. Pull yarn through stitch and loop on hook. Round 2 complete.

Now try a few patterns that are worked in increasing joined rounds on the following pages!

Nifty Placemat

This project is worked from the center outward in joined rounds that increase to create a flat circle. Each round has a different stitch pattern, creating stripes of solid and open fabric.

Tip: Plant fibers (like cotton) are best for this project if the placemats will be used in the dining room. While it may be a bit tricky at first, using a small hook size (like the G-6/4.0 mm referenced) will create a tight, even fabric that's very durable.

SIZE/FINISHED MEASUREMENTS
11 in. (27.94 cm) across

YARN
Cascade Yarns Nifty Cotton, Medium weight #4 (100% cotton; 185 yd./169.5 m; 3.5 oz./100 g hank):
- Natural: 1 hank (80 yd./73.15 m make one placemat)

Also try: Knit Picks Dishie, Bernat Handicrafter, Lily Sugar 'n Cream

HOOK & OTHER MATERIALS
- US size G-6 (4.0 mm) crochet hook
- Scissors
- Yarn needle
- Measuring tape
- Stitch markers

GAUGE
Gauge is not crucial for this project.

STITCH KEY
ch = chain
dc = double crochet
sl st = slip stitch

■ INSTRUCTIONS

Round 1 (right side): Ch 4 (first dc + base ch), work 11 dc into fourth ch from hook, sl st into top of first dc to join—12 dc.

Round 2: Ch 5 (first dc + ch-2 space, here and throughout), [(dc, ch2) into next st] 11 times, sl st into beginning ch-2 space to join—36 sts; 12 dc + 12 ch-2 spaces.

Round 3: Ch 3 (first dc, here and throughout), work 3 dc into same ch-2 space, work 4 dc into next 11 ch-2 spaces, sl st into top of first dc to join—48 dc.

Round 4: Ch 5, skip 1 st, [(dc, ch 2) into next st, skip 1 st] 23 times, sl st into beginning ch-2 space to join—72 sts; 24 dc + 24 ch-2 spaces.

Round 5: Ch 3, work 2 dc into same ch-2 space, [work 3 dc into next ch-2 space] 23 times, sl st into top of first dc to join—72 dc.

Round 6: Ch 5, skip 1 st, [(dc, ch 2) into next st, skip 1 st] 35 times, sl st into beginning ch-2 space to join—108 sts; 36 dc + 36 ch-2 spaces.

Round 7: Ch 3, work 2 dc into same ch-2 space, [work 3 dc into next ch-2 space] 35 times, sl st into top of first dc to join—108 dc.

Round 8: Ch 3, skip 1 st, [(dc, ch 2) into next st, skip 1 st] 53 times, sl st into beginning ch-2 space to join—162 sts; 54 dc + 54 ch-2 spaces.

Round 9: Ch 3, work 2 dc into same ch-2 space, work 2 dc into next ch-2 space, [work 3 dc into next ch-2 space, work 2 dc into next ch-2 space] 26 times, sl st into top of first dc to join, fasten off—135 dc.

Sew in ends; trim excess.

Stitch Key

⬭ Chain

● Slip Stitch

丅 Double Crochet

Nifty Placemat Stitch Diagram

Stitch diagram not to full pattern scale.

Floral Motif Coaster

This center outward pattern is worked with just a few joined rounds. The fabric is created using Bobble stitches; the Bobble is a complex stitch variation that takes a bit of extra care to work up.

Tip: Leave your beginning and ending tail ends a bit long so that you can weave or sew them together and knot when finished to really secure them down.

SIZES/FINISHED MEASUREMENTS
5.5 in. (13.97 cm) across

YARN
Lion Brand Yarn 24/7 Cotton, Medium weight #4 (100% mercerized cotton; 186 yd./170 m; 3.5 oz./100 g skein):
- Camel: 1 skein (30 yd./27.43 m make one floral coaster)

Also try: Knit Picks Dishie, Bernat Handicrafter, Peaches & Creme

HOOK & OTHER MATERIALS
- US size G-6 (4.0 mm) crochet hook
- Scissors
- Yarn needle
- Measuring tape
- Stitch markers

GAUGE
Gauge is not crucial for this project.

STITCH KEY
ch = chain
sl st = slip stitch
sc = single crochet

SPECIALTY STITCHES & TECHNIQUES
Bobble: [Yarn over, insert hook into space, yarn over, pull through st, yarn over, pull through 2 loops on hook] 3 times, yarn over, pull through all 4 loops on hook.

NOTE
Floral motif is worked in joined rounds, from the center outward.

INSTRUCTIONS

Round 1 (right side): Ch 2 (counts as base chain not a st, here and throughout), [Bobble, ch 3] 6 times into second ch from hook, sl st into first ch-3 space to join—24 sts; 6 Bobbles + 6 ch-3 spaces.

Round 2: Ch 2, [(Bobble, ch 3, Bobble) into ch-3 space, ch 3] 6 times, sl st into first ch-3 space to join—48 sts; 12 Bobbles + 12 ch-3 spaces.

Round 3: Ch 2, [(Bobble, ch 3, Bobble) into ch-3 space, (ch 3, Bobble, ch 3) into next ch-3 space] 6 times, sl st into first ch-3 space to join—72 sts; 18 Bobbles + 18 ch-3 spaces.

Round 4: Ch 1 (not a st), (2 sc, ch 1, 2 sc) into each ch-3 space around, sl st into first sc to join, fasten off—90 sts; 72 sc + 18 ch.

Weave in ends; trim excess.

Stitch Key

⬭ Chain

● Slip Stitch

+ Single Crochet

◈ Bobble

Floral Motif Coaster Stitch Diagram

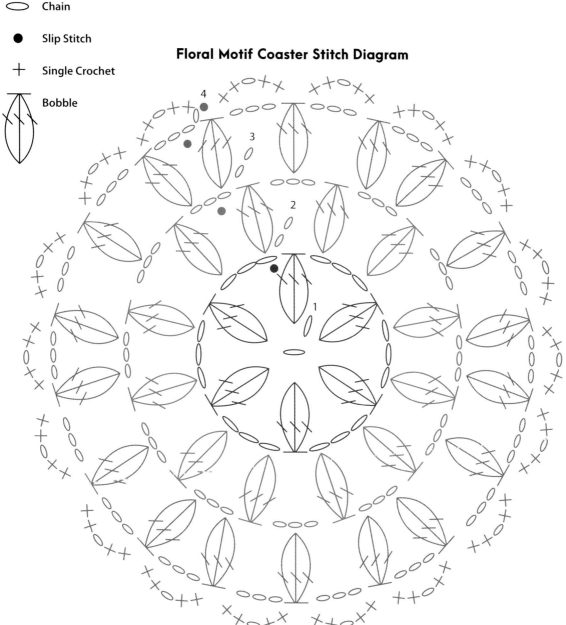

Chunky
Motif Blanket

You'll crochet each center-out motif first, and then join each one together with single crochet once you have them all finished. This motif begins in a circle, but the last round has a special pattern repeat that turns it into a square shape.

Tip: Sew down ends for each motif as they are complete to make the finishing process much easier.

SIZE/FINISHED MEASUREMENTS
37.5 in. wide x 45 in. tall (95.25 cm x 114.30 cm)

YARN
Bernat Softee Chunky, Super Bulky weight #6 (100% acrylic; 431 yd./394 m per 14 oz./400 g skein):
- Teal (Color A): 2 skeins
- Natural (Color B): 1 skein

Also try: Red Heart Soft Essentials, Knit Picks Brava Bulky, Caron Colorama O'Go

HOOK & OTHER MATERIALS
- US size L-11 (8.0 mm) crochet hook
- Scissors
- Yarn needle
- Measuring tape
- Stitch markers

GAUGE
1 motif = 7.5 in. x 7.5 in. (19.05 cm x 19.05 cm)

STITCH KEY
ch = chain
sc = single crochet
sl st = slip stitch
dc = double crochet

NOTES
- Each motif is worked individually and then joined together once complete.
- To alter blanket size, create any number of squares as desired and join accordingly.

■ INSTRUCTIONS

Motif (make 30)

Round 1 (right side): With Color A, ch 4 (first dc + base ch), work 11 dc into fourth ch from hook, sl st into top of first st to join—12 dc.

Round 2: Ch 3 (first dc, here and throughout), dc into same st, [work 2 dc into next st] 11 times, sl st into top of first st to join, fasten off Color A—24 dc.

Round 3: With Color B, ch 3, skip 1 st, [work 3 dc into next st, skip 1 st] 11 times, work 2 dc into first st of round, sl st into top of first st to join—36 dc.

Round 4: Ch 3, (2 dc, ch 2, 3 dc) into space between first and second dc sts, skip 3 sts, [work 3 dc into space between sts, skip 3 sts, work 3 dc into space between sts, (3 dc, ch 2, 3 dc) into space between sts] 3 times, skip 3 sts, work 3 dc into space between sts, skip 3 sts, work 3 dc into space between sts, sl st into top of first st to join, fasten off—56 sts; 48 dc + 4 ch-2 spaces.

Joining

Arrange motifs into 6 rows of 5 motifs (ensure all motifs are facing the right side):

Row 1 (right side): Hold any 2 adjacent motifs with back of fabric together. With Color A, begin at first ch-2 corner, sc through both thicknesses across both motifs. Continue across remaining 4 pairs of motifs until last ch-2 space is met. Fasten off.

Repeat Row 1 for each horizontal join (70 sc per row).

Rotate throw and repeat Row 1 for each vertical join (84 sc per row).

Border

With right side of blanket facing, attach yarn into any unworked ch-2 corner space.

Round 1 (right side): With Color A, ch 1 (not a st), work 1 sc into each unworked st around, sl st into top of first st to join—308 sc.

Finishing

Sew in ends; trim excess.

Chunky Motif Blanket Stitch Diagram

Stitch Key

◯ Chain

● Slip Stitch

┬ Double Crochet

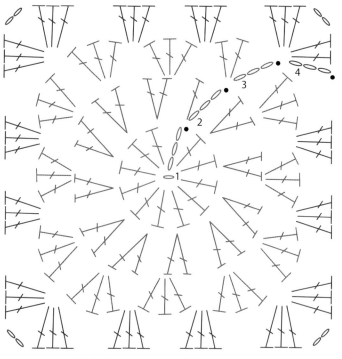

Stitch diagram not to full pattern scale.

INCREASING CONTINUOUS ROUNDS

Increasing rounds don't have to join. In fact, you can simply work in a continuous spiral to eliminate the joining seam! It's important to note that these should always begin with small stitches in the beginning of the first round only; that way, the first stitches in the next round can be worked on top without a huge gap.

Increasing continuous rounds in single crochet, Round 1.

Increasing continuous rounds in single crochet, Round 2.

TUTORIAL: INCREASING CONTINUOUS ROUNDS

Increasing Continuous Rounds in Single Crochet Stitch Diagram

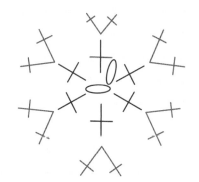

Stitch diagram not to full pattern scale.

Stitch Key

⬭ Chain

✝ Single Crochet

⤬ 2 Single Crochet into 1 Stitch

1. Chain 2 (base chain only).

2. Single crochet into 2nd chain from hook.

3. Place stitch marker into both loops.

4. Work 5 single crochet into 2nd chain from hook (6 total). Round 1 complete.

5. Work 2 single crochet into each stitch around (12 total). Round 2 complete.

6. Place stitch marker into both loops of first single crochet.

7. Work 2 single crochet into each stitch around (12 total).

Now try a few patterns that are worked in increasing continuous rounds on the following pages!

Two-Toned Baskets

This project is worked from the bottom upward in a continuous spiral circle, adding stitches with every new round until you reach the desired circumference. Baskets are a great way to learn how to work in rounds of crochet, especially since you'll get a lot of practice!

Tip: *Gauge and size are not crucial for this project; you can use other weights, colors, and types of yarn to make these!*

SIZES/FINISHED MEASUREMENTS
Small: 25 in. (63.5 cm) around (12.5 in./30.48 cm flat) x 12.5 in. (31.75 cm) tall (8 in./20.32 cm standing)
Medium: 37 in. (93.98 cm) around (18.5 in./46.99 cm flat) x 18.5 in. (46.99 cm) tall (11 in./27.94 cm standing)
Large: 50 in. (127 cm) around (25 in./63.5 cm flat) x 23.5 in. (23.5 cm) tall (15 in./38.1 cm standing)

YARN
Bernat Softee Chunky, Super Bulky weight #6 (100% acrylic; 431 yd./394 m per 14 oz./400 g skein):
- Natural (Color A): 1 (1, 2) skein
Bernat Softee Chunky, Super Bulky weight #6 (100% acrylic; 108 yd./99 m per 3.5 oz./100 g skein):
- Seagreen (Color B): 1 skein or less
Also try: Red Heart Soft Essentials, Knit Picks Brava Bulky, Caron Colorama O'Go

HOOK & OTHER MATERIALS
- US size L-J/11 (8.0 mm) crochet hook
- Scissors
- Yarn needle
- Measuring tape
- Stitch markers

GAUGE
17 sts = 7 in. (17.78 cm), 4 rows = 1.5 in. (3.81 cm)

STITCH KEY
ch = chain
sc = single crochet
sl st = slip stitch

NOTES
- Rounds are not joined; work each round in a continuous circle.
- When working continuous rounds, place one stitch marker into the top of the first stitch in each round to mark progress.

■ INSTRUCTIONS

All sizes

Round 1 (right side): With Color A, ch 2 (not a st), work 6 sc into second ch from hook—6 sc.

Round 2: Work 2 sc into each st around—12 sc.

Round 3: [Work 2 sc into 1 st, sc into following] 6 times—18 sc.

Round 4: [Work 2 sc into 1 st, sc into following 2 sts] 6 times—24 sc.

Round 5: [Work 2 sc into 1 st, sc into following 3 sts] 6 times—30 sc.

Round 6: [Work 2 sc into 1 st, sc into following 4 sts] 6 times—36 sc.

Round 7: [Work 2 sc into 1 st, sc into following 5 sts] 6 times—42 sc.

Round 8: [Work 2 sc into 1 st, sc into following 6 sts] 6 times—48 sc.

Round 9: [Work 2 sc into 1 st, sc into following 7 sts] 6 times—54 sc.

Round 10: [Work 2 sc into 1 st, sc into following 8 sts] 6 times—60 sc.

Follow instructions for individual size only.

Small

Rounds 11–30: Work 1 sc into each st around—60 sc.

Round 31: Fasten off Color A, attach Color B, [ch 20 (handle), skip 10 sts, sc into following 20 sts] 2 times—80 sts; 40 ch + 40 sc.

Rounds 32–34: Work 1 sc into each st around—80 sc. Sl st into following st. Fasten off.

Medium

Round 11: [Work 2 sc into 1 st, sc into following 9 sts] 6 times—66 sc.

Round 12: [Work 2 sc into 1 st, sc into following 10 sts] 6 times—72 sc.

Round 13: [Work 2 sc into 1 st, sc into following 11 sts] 6 times—78 sc.

Round 14: [Work 2 sc into 1 st, sc into following 12 sts] 6 times—84 sc.
Round 15: [Work 2 sc into 1 st, sc into following 13 sts] 6 times—90 sc.
Rounds 16–45: Work 1 sc into each st around—90 sc.
Round 46: Fasten off Color A, attach Color B, [ch 20 (handle), skip 10 sts, sc into following 35 sts] 2 times—110 sts; 40 ch + 70 sc.
Rounds 47–49: Work 1 sc into each st around—110 sc.
Sl st into following st. Fasten off.

Large

Round 11: [Work 2 sc into 1 st, sc into following 9 sts] 6 times—66 sc.
Round 12: [Work 2 sc into 1 st, sc into following 10 sts] 6 times—72 sc.
Round 13: [Work 2 sc into 1 st, sc into following 11 sts] 6 times—78 sc.
Round 14: [Work 2 sc into 1 st, sc into following 12 sts] 6 times—84 sc.
Round 15: [Work 2 sc into 1 st, sc into following 13 sts] 6 times—90 sc.

Round 16: [Work 2 sc into 1 st, sc into following 14 sts] 6 times—96 sc.
Round 17: [Work 2 sc into 1 st, sc into following 15 sts] 6 times—102 sc.
Round 18: [Work 2 sc into 1 st, sc into following 16 sts] 6 times—108 sc.
Round 19: [Work 2 sc into 1 st, sc into following 17 sts] 6 times—114 sc.
Round 20: [Work 2 sc into 1 st, sc into following 18 sts] 6 times—120 sc.
Rounds 21–60: Work 1 sc into each st around—120 sc.
Round 61: Fasten off Color A, attach Color B, [ch 20 (handle), skip 10 sts, sc into following 50 sts] 2 times—140 sts; 40 ch + 100 sc.
Rounds 62–64: Work 1 sc into each st around—140 sc.
Sl st into following st. Fasten off.

Finishing (all sizes)
Sew in all ends; trim excess.

Stitch Key

⬭ Chain

╋ Single Crochet

⋋⋌ 2 Single Crochet into 1 Stitch

Two-Toned Baskets Stitch Diagram

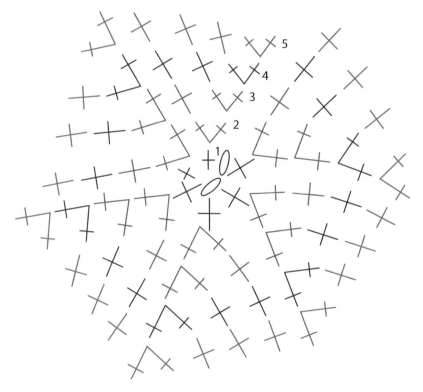

Stitch diagram not to full pattern scale.

Basic Beanie

This super basic beanie is worked from the top of the head down to the brim in continuous rounds. Just like the Two-Toned Baskets, you'll work in continuous rounds that don't join, but now you'll try that technique with a larger stitch (the half double crochet). Note that the slip stitch is used in the instructions only once here as a final step, just to even out the end of the last round of work.

Tip: Gauge and size are important for this project, so use the yarn indicated or substitute with another yarn of the same weight and type that is similar to match the stitch and row gauge as closely as possible.

SIZES/FINISHED MEASUREMENTS
16 in. around x 6.75 in. tall (40.54 cm x 17.15 cm)
18 in. around x 7.5 in. tall (45.72 cm x 19.05 cm)
20 in. around x 7.75 in. tall (50.08 cm x 19.69 cm)
22 in. around x 8 in. tall (55.88 cm x 20.32 cm)
24 in. around x 8.5 in. tall (60.96 cm x 21.59 cm)

YARN
Cascade Yarns Friday Harbor, Medium weight #4 (80% merino wool, 20% silk; 219 yd./200 m per 3.5 oz./100 g hank):
- Turquoise Pebble: 1 hank (enough for any size)

Also try: Universal Yarn Deluxe Worsted Tweed Superwash, Knit Picks Wool of the Andes Tweed, Plymouth Yarn Encore Worsted Tweed

HOOK & OTHER MATERIALS
- US size J-10 (6.0 mm) crochet hook
- Scissors
- Yarn needle
- Measuring tape
- Stitch markers

GAUGE
12.5 hdc sts = 4 in. (10.16 cm), 9 hdc rows = 4 in. (10.16 cm)
12.5 sc sts = 4 in. (10.16 cm), 3 sc rows = 1 in. (2.54 cm)

STITCH KEY
ch = chain
sc = single crochet
hdc = half double crochet
sl st = slip stitch

NOTES
- Rounds are not joined; work each round in a continuous circle.
- When working continuous rounds, place one stitch marker into the top of the first stitch in each round to mark progress.

INSTRUCTIONS

All Sizes

Round 1 (right side): Ch 2 (not a st), work 2 sc and 8 hdc into second ch from hook—10 sts; 2 sc + 8 hdc.

Round 2: Work 2 hdc into each st around—20 hdc.

Round 3: [Work 2 hdc into 1 st, hdc into following] 10 times—30 hdc.

Round 4: [Work 2 hdc into 1 st, hdc into following 2 sts] 10 times—40 hdc.

Round 5: [Work 2 hdc into 1 st, hdc into following 3 sts] 10 times—50 hdc.

Follow instructions for individual size only.

16 in. (40.54 cm)

Rounds 6–13: Work 1 hdc into each st around—50 hdc.

Rounds 14–17: Work 1 sc into each st around—50 sc.

Sl st into following st. Fasten off.

18 in. (45.72 cm)

Round 6: [Work 2 hdc into 1 st, hdc into following 9 sts] 5 times—55 hdc.

Rounds 7–14: Work 1 hdc into each st around—55 hdc.

Rounds 15–17: Work 1 sc into each st around—55 sc.

Sl st into following st. Fasten off.

20 in. (50.06 cm)

Round 6: [Work 2 hdc into 1 st, hdc into following 4 sts] 10 times—60 hdc.

Rounds 7–15: Work 1 hdc into each st around—60 hdc.

Rounds 16–18: Work 1 sc into each st around—60 sc.

Sl st into following st. Fasten off.

22 in. (55.88 cm)

Round 6: [Work 2 hdc into 1 st, hdc into following 4 sts] 10 times—60 hdc.

Round 7: [Work 2 hdc into 1 st, hdc into following 9 sts] 6 times—66 hdc.

Rounds 8–16: Work 1 hdc into each st around—66 hdc.

Rounds 17–19: Work 1 sc into each st around—66 sc.

Sl st into following st. Fasten off.

24 in. (60.96 cm)

Round 6: [Work 2 hdc into 1 st, hdc into following 4 sts] 10 times—60 hdc.

Round 7: [Work 2 hdc into 1 st, hdc into following 5 sts] 10 times—70 hdc.

Round 8: [Work 2 hdc into 1 st, hdc into following 34 sts] 2 times—72 hdc.

Rounds 9–17: Work 1 hdc into each st around—72 hdc.

Rounds 18–20: Work 1 sc into each st around—72 sc.

Sl st into following st. Fasten off.

Finishing (All Sizes)

Sew in all ends; trim excess.

Basic Beanie Stitch Diagram

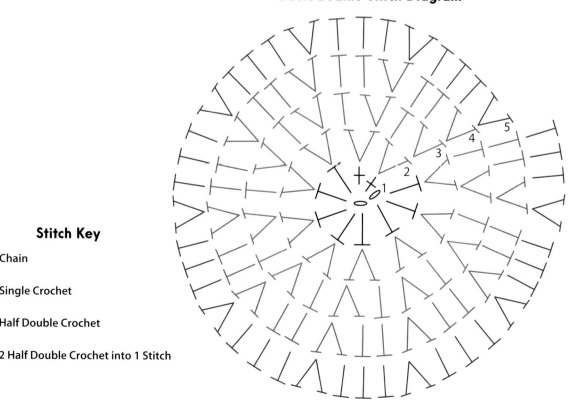

Stitch Key

⬭ Chain

✛ Single Crochet

⊤ Half Double Crochet

⋁ 2 Half Double Crochet into 1 Stitch

Stitch diagram not to full pattern scale.

Crochet Complex Combinations

This section incorporates rows, tubes, and rounds together to make even more combinations of crochet projects possible.

Each pattern works in a way you've already learned but has an element that gives the design a special feature and makes it a bit more challenging.

Basic Slouch

This project is worked entirely in rows, creating one big rectangle of fabric. Once the height of all rows measures the hat circumference (around), you'll join the first and last rows together using slip stitches to create a tube. Then you'll cinch up just one side of the tube to create a slouchy-looking beanie hat!

Tip: Measure the height of your rows as you go to get a hat that fits perfectly every time! This type of hat construction allows you to try different yarns and still get a great fit.

SIZES/FINISHED MEASUREMENTS
17.5 in. around x 7.5 in. tall (44.45 cm x 19.05 cm)
18.5 in. around x 9 in. tall (46.99 cm x 22.86 cm)
20 in. around x 10.5 in. tall (50.80 cm x 26.67 cm)
21.5 in. around x 12 in. tall (54.61 cm x 30.48 cm)
23.25 in. around x 13.5 in. tall (59.06 cm x 34.29 cm)

YARN
Lion Brand Yarn Wool Ease, Medium weight #4 (80% acrylic, 20% wool; 197 yd./180 m; 3 oz./85 g skein):
- Linen: 1 (1, 1, 2, 2) skeins

Also try: Loops & Threads Impeccable Tweed, Premier Yarns Just Worsted, Red Heart Hygge Charm

HOOK & OTHER MATERIALS
- US size H-8 (5.0 mm) crochet hook
- Scissors
- Yarn needle
- Measuring tape
- Stitch markers

GAUGE
10 pattern sts = 3 in. (7.62 cm), 10 pattern rows = 4 in. (10.16 cm)

STITCH KEY
ch = chain
sc = single crochet
hdc = half double crochet
sl st = slip stitch

NOTES
- For the best fit, measure around at forehead and follow pattern size that is the closest match.
- Hat is worked in two sections: Hat Body, Hat Top.

■ INSTRUCTIONS

17.5 (18.5, 20, 21.5, 23.25) in. (44.45, 46.99, 50.80, 54.61, 59.06 cm)

Hat Body

Ch 27 (32, 37, 42, 47).

Row 1: Skip 2 chs (not a st), work 1 hdc into each ch across—25 (30, 35, 40, 45) hdc.

Row 2: Ch 2, (not a st), turn, work 1 hdc into each st across—25 (30, 35, 40, 45) hdc.

Repeat Row 2 until 44 (46, 50, 54, 58) rows complete.

Hold Row 1 together with last row completed. Sl st both thicknesses together evenly—44 (46, 50, 54, 58) sl sts.

Sl st seam creates back side of fabric; turn so that sl st seam is on inside. Do not fasten off. Continue to Hat Top.

Hat Top

Round 1: Ch 1 (not a st), work 1 sc into side of every other hdc st around, sl st into top of first sc to join, fasten off 30 in. (76.2 cm) tail—22 (23, 25, 27, 29) sc.

Weave 30 in. (76.2 cm) tail into every other sc st from Row 1 of Hat Top. Pull tail until Hat Top is closed. Knot; fasten off.

Finishing

Sew in ends; trim excess.

Stitch Key

⊝ Chain

⊤ Half Double Crochet

Basic Slouch Stitch Diagram

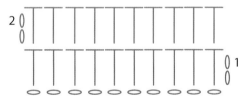

Stitch diagram not to full pattern scale.

Dishie Basket

Using only chains and single crochet, this basket is worked from the bottom up in three parts. The bottom is worked back and forth in rows (creating a square—no increasing rounds!). While rounds of crochet typically create a distinct front and back side of fabric, you'll turn after each round joined at the beginning of the sides to get reversible fabric. Change color and add simple single crochet in joined rounds (without turning) to finish off this project.

Tip: Gauge and size are not crucial for this project, so try this pattern with other weights, types, and colors of yarn to taste!

SIZE/FINISHED MEASUREMENTS
One size: 6 in. x 6 in. (15.24 cm x 15.24 cm) bottom,
    25 in. around x 6 in. tall (63.25 cm x 15.24 cm)

YARN
Knit Picks Dishie, Medium weight #4 (100% cotton; 190 yd./173 m; 3.5 oz./100 g skein):
- Linen (Color A): 1 skein
- Swan (Color B): 1 skein

Also try: Lion Brand Yarn Pima Cotton, Premier Yarns Just Cotton, Women's Institute Home Cotton

HOOK & OTHER MATERIALS
- US size G-8 (4.0 mm) crochet hook
- Scissors
- Yarn needle
- Measuring tape
- Stitch markers

GAUGE
16.76 sts = 4 in. (10.16 cm), 20 rows = 4 in. (10.16 cm)

STITCH KEY
ch = chain
sc = single crochet
sl st = slip stitch

■ INSTRUCTIONS

Bottom
With Color A, Ch 26.

Row 1: Skip 1 ch (not a st, here and throughout), work 1 sc into each st across—25 sc.

Row 2: Ch 1, turn, work 1 sc into each st across—25 sc.
Repeat Row 2 until 30 rows complete. Do not fasten off. Continue on to Sides.

Sides
Round 1: Ch 1 (not a st), turn to work into left end rows, place 1 sc into each sc end row, turn to work across Row 1, place 1 sc into each sc st, turn to work across right end rows, place 1 sc into each sc end row, turn to work across Row 30, place 1 sc into each sc st, sl st into top of first sc to join—110 sc.

Round 2: Ch 1 (not a st), turn, work 1 sc into each st around, sl st into top of first sc to join—110 sc.
Repeat Round 2 until 20 rounds complete. Fasten off Color A, attach Color B.

Round 21 (right side): Ch 1 (not a st), work 1 sc into each st around, sl st into top of first sc to join—110 sc.

Repeat Round 21 until 30 rounds complete. Fasten off.

Finishing
Weave in ends; trim excess.

Dishie Basket Stitch Diagram

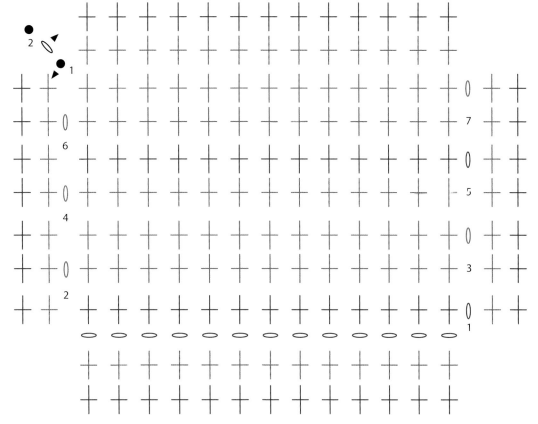

Stitch Key

⬯ Chain

● Slip Stitch

✛ Single Crochet

◀ Turn, direction

Stitch diagram not to full pattern scale.

Triplicity Tote Set

These tote bags all begin with the same stitch pattern, and increasing the stitch pattern per round is how each tote gets larger. While slip stitches are how we join rounds of work, they can also help move the starting location of your next round, which can make pattern instructions easier to work up and follow.

Tip: Gauge and size are not crucial for this pattern. Experiment with cotton yarns (and cotton blends) in other weights for the same great end result!

YARN

Patons Hempster, Light weight #3 (55% hemp, 45% cotton; 190 yd./174 m; 3.5 oz./100 g skein):
- Wine Tote—Spice: 1 skein
- Medium Tote—Sepia: 2 skeins
- Large Tote—Ecru: 2 skeins

Also try: Stylecraft Craft Cotton, Yeoman Yarns DK Soft Cotton, Knit Picks CotLin

HOOK & OTHER MATERIALS
- US size G-6 (4.0 mm) crochet hook
- Scissors
- Yarn needle
- Measuring tape
- Stitch markers

GAUGE

19 pattern sts = 4 in. (10.16 cm), 8 pattern rows = 4 in. (10.16 cm)

SIZES/FINISHED MEASUREMENTS

Wine Tote: 11 in. (27.94 cm) around (5.5 in./13.97 cm flat) x 13 in. (33.02 cm) tall (without handles)
Medium Tote: 30 in. (76.2 cm) around (15 in./38.10 flat) x 15 in. (38.01 cm) tall (without handles)
Large Tote: 38 in. (96.52 cm) around (19 in./48.26 cm flat) x 15 in. (38.01 cm) tall (without handles)

STITCH KEY

ch = chain
sl st = slip stitch
sc = single crochet
dc = double crochet

NOTE

Tote is worked in one solid piece, from the bottom up.

■ INSTRUCTIONS

All Sizes

Round 1 (right side): Ch 5 (first dc + ch 1+ base ch), [2 dc, ch 1] 5 times into fifth ch from hook, dc into fifth ch from hook, sl st into top of first st to join—18 sts; 12 dc + 6 ch-1 spaces.

Round 2: Sl st over to ch-1 space, ch 4 (first dc + ch 1, here and throughout), work 2 dc into same ch-1 space, ch 1, (2 dc, ch 1, 2 dc, ch 1) into next 5 ch-1 spaces, dc into first ch-1 space of round, sl st into top of first st to join—36 sts; 24 dc + 12 ch-1 spaces.

Round 3: Sl st over to ch-1 space, ch 4, work 2 dc into same ch-1 space, ch 1, work 2 dc into next ch-1 space, ch 1, [(2 dc, ch 1, 2 dc, ch 1) into next ch-1 space, (2 dc, ch 1) into following ch-1 space] 5 times, dc into first ch-1 space of round, sl st into top of first st to join—54 sts; 36 dc + 18 ch-1 spaces.

Wine Tote size only: Do not fasten off. Continue to individual instructions.

Round 4: Sl st over to ch-1 space, ch 4, work 2 dc into same ch-1 space, ch 1, (2 dc into next ch-1 space, ch 1) 2 times, [(2 dc, ch 1, 2 dc, ch 1) into next ch-1 space, (2 dc, ch 1) into following 2 ch-1 spaces] 5 times, dc into first ch-1 space of round, sl st into top of first st to join—72 sts; 48 dc + 24 ch-1 spaces.

Round 5: Sl st over to ch-1 space, ch 4, work 2 dc into same ch-1 space, ch 1, (2 dc into next ch-1 space, ch 1) 3 times, [(2 dc, ch 1, 2 dc, ch 1) into next ch-1 space, (2 dc, ch 1) into following 3 ch-1 spaces] 5 times, dc into first ch-1 space of round, sl st into top of first st to join—90 sts; 60 dc + 30 ch-1 spaces.

Round 6: Sl st over to ch-1 space, ch 4, work 2 dc into same ch-1 space, ch 1, (2 dc into next ch-1 space, ch 1) 4 times, [(2 dc, ch 1, 2 dc, ch 1) into next ch-1 space, (2 dc, ch 1) into following 4 ch-1 spaces] 5 times, dc into first ch-1 space of round, sl st into top of first st to join—108 sts; 72 dc + 36 ch-1 spaces.

Round 7: Sl st over to ch-1 space, ch 4, work 2 dc into same ch-1 space, ch 1, (2 dc into next ch-1 space, ch 1) 5 times, [(2 dc, ch 1, 2 dc, ch 1) into next ch-1 space, (2 dc, ch 1) into following 5 ch-1 spaces] 5 times, dc into first ch-1 space of round, sl st into top of first st to join—126 sts; 84 dc + 42 ch-1 spaces.

Round 8: Sl st over to ch-1 space, ch 4, work 2 dc into same ch-1 space, ch 1, (2 dc into next ch-1 space, ch 1) 6 times, [(2 dc, ch 1, 2 dc, ch 1) into next ch-1 space, (2 dc, ch 1) into following 6 ch-1 spaces] 5 times, dc into first ch-1 space of round, sl st into top of first st to join—144 sts; 96 dc + 48 ch-1 spaces.

Medium Tote size only: Do not fasten off. Continue to individual instructions.

Round 9: Sl st over to ch-1 space, ch 4, work 2 dc into same ch-1 space, ch 1, (2 dc into next ch-1 space, ch 1) 7 times, [(2 dc, ch 1, 2 dc, ch 1) into next ch-1 space, (2 dc, ch 1) into following 7 ch-1 spaces] 5

times, dc into first ch-1 space of round, sl st into top of first st to join—162 sts; 108 dc + 54 ch-1 spaces.

Round 10: Sl st over to ch-1 space, ch 4, work 2 dc into same ch-1 space, ch 1, (2 dc into next ch-1 space, ch 1) 8 times, [(2 dc, ch 1, 2 dc, ch 1) into next ch-1 space, (2 dc, ch 1) into following 8 ch-1 spaces] 5 times, dc into first ch-1 space of round, sl st into top of first st to join—180 sts; 120 dc + 60 ch-1 spaces.

Do not fasten off. Continue to Large instructions.

Wine Tote

Round 4: Sl st over to ch-1 space, ch 3 (first dc), dc into same ch-1 space, ch 1, [(2 dc, ch 1) into next ch-1 space] 17 times, sl st into top of first st to join—54 sts; 36 dc + 18 ch-1 spaces.

Repeat Round 4 until 25 rounds complete.

Round 26: Sl st over to ch-1 space, ch 1 (not a st, here and throughout), work 2 sc into first 3 ch-1 spaces, ch 25 (handle), skip 3 ch-1 spaces, work 2 sc into each of next 6 ch-1 spaces, ch 25 (handle), skip 3 ch-1 spaces, work 2 sc into last 3 ch-1 spaces, sl st into top of first st to join—74 sts; 24 sc + 50 ch.

Round 27: Ch 1, work 1 sc into each st around, sl st into top of first st to join—74 sc.

Repeat Round 27 until 29 rounds complete, fasten off.

Medium Tote

Round 9: Sl st over to ch-1 space, ch 3 (first dc), dc into same ch-1 space, ch 1, [(2 dc, ch 1) into next ch-1 space] 47 times, sl st into top of first st to join—144 sts; 96 dc + 48 ch-1 spaces.

Repeat Round 9 until 28 rounds complete.

Round 29: Sl st over to ch-1 space, ch 1 (not a st, here and throughout), work 2 sc into first 8 ch-1 spaces, ch 75 (handle), skip 8 ch-1 spaces, work 2 sc into each of next 16 ch-1 spaces, ch 75 (handle), skip 8 ch-1 spaces, work 2 sc into last 8 ch-1 spaces, sl st into top of first st to join—214 sts; 64 sc + 150 ch.

Round 30: Ch 1, work 1 sc into each st around, sl st into top of first st to join—214 sc.

Repeat Round 30 until 34 rounds complete, fasten off.

Large Tote

Round 11: Sl st over to ch-1 space, ch 3 (first dc), dc into same ch-1 space, ch 1, [(2 dc, ch 1) into next ch-1 space] 59 times, sl st into top of first st to join—180 sts; 120 dc + 60 ch-1 spaces.

Repeat Round 11 until 28 rounds complete.

Round 29: Sl st over to ch-1 space, ch 1 (not a st, here and throughout), work 2 sc into first 10 ch-1 spaces, ch 75 (handle), skip 10 ch-1 spaces, work 2 sc into each of next 20 ch-1 spaces, ch 75 (handle), skip 10 ch-1 spaces, work 2 sc into last 10 ch-1 spaces, sl st into top of first st to join—230 sts; 80 sc + 150 ch.

Round 30: Ch 1, work 1 sc into each st around, sl st into top of first st to join—230 sc.

Repeat Round 30 until 34 rounds complete, fasten off.

Finishing

All sizes: Weave in ends; trim excess.

Stitch Key

◯   Chain

●   Slip Stitch

⊤   Double Crochet

ᐯ   2 Double Crochet into 1 Stitch

Triplicity Tote Stitch Diagram

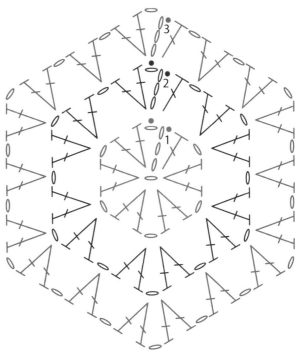

Stitch diagram not to full pattern scale.

Pentagon Banner

Working in joined rounds can create more shapes than just circles when you follow a different pattern of stitch repeats—like this pentagon shape. Slip stitches are used to join each round here, but they are also used to move the starting position of each round.

Tip: Gauge and size are not crucial for this project, so have fun with different yarn fibers and colors! Leave your beginning and ending tails long enough on each motif to sew and knot together as you go.

SIZES/FINISHED MEASUREMENTS
Motif = 4.5 in. (11.43 cm) across, 5 in. (12.7 cm) tall
Banner as shown = 36 in. (91.44 cm) long

YARN
Red Heart Creme de la Creme, Medium weight #4 (100% combed cotton; 125 yd./114.30 m per 2.5 oz./ 70 g skein):
- Dark Linen: 1 skein

Also try: Knit Picks Dishie, Bernat Handicrafter, Lion Brand Yarn 24/7 Cotton

HOOK & OTHER MATERIALS
- US size G-6 (4.0 mm) crochet hook
- Scissors
- Yarn needle
- Measuring tape
- Stitch markers

GAUGE
Gauge is not crucial for this project.

STITCH KEY
ch = chain
sl st = slip stitch
sc = single crochet
dc = double crochet

NOTES
- Any yarn weight/type may be used, as desired.
- Be sure to use an odd number of motifs for a U shape when hanging; even numbers will create a V shape when hanging.

■ INSTRUCTIONS

Motif (make 5)

Round 1 (right side): Ch 4 (first dc + base ch), dc, ch 2, [2 dc, ch 2] 4 times into fourth ch from hook, sl st to top of first dc to join—20 sts; 10 dc + 10 ch.

Round 2: Sl st until first ch-2 space reached, ch 3 (first dc, here and throughout), (dc, ch 2, 2 dc) into same space, ch 1, [2 dc, ch 2, 2 dc, ch 1] into next 4 ch-2 spaces, sl st to top of first dc to join—35 sts; 20 dc + 15 ch.

Round 3: Sl st until first ch-2 space reached, ch 3, (dc, ch 2, 2 dc) into same space, ch 1, (2 dc, ch 1) into next ch-1 space, [(2 dc, ch 2, 2 dc) into next ch-2 space, ch 1, (2 dc, ch 1) into next ch-1 space] 4 times, sl st to top of first dc to join—50 sts; 30 dc + 20 ch.

Round 4: Sl st until first ch-2 space reached, ch 3, (dc, ch 2, 2 dc) into same space, ch 1, (2 dc, ch 1) into next 2 ch-1 spaces, [(2 dc, ch 2, 2 dc) into next ch-2 space, ch 1, (2 dc, ch 1) into next 2 ch-1 spaces] 4 times, sl st to top of first dc to join, sl st until first ch-2 space reached, fasten off—65 sts; 40 dc + 25 ch.

Joining

Row 1 (RS): Ch 15, work (2 sc, ch 1) into each ch-space across one motif side, ch 4 between each motif. Ch 15; fasten off—50 sc + 70 ch.

Fringe

For each center ch-2 space per Round 4, plus beginning and ending chs on Row 1 of Joining: Cut 5 pieces of yarn measuring 6 in. (15.24 cm) each, fold in half evenly, loop fold through ch-2 space, pull ends through fold to knot.

Finishing

Sew in all ends; trim excess.

Pentagon Banner Stitch Diagram

Stitch Key

⊙ Chain

● Slip Stitch

┬ Double Crochet

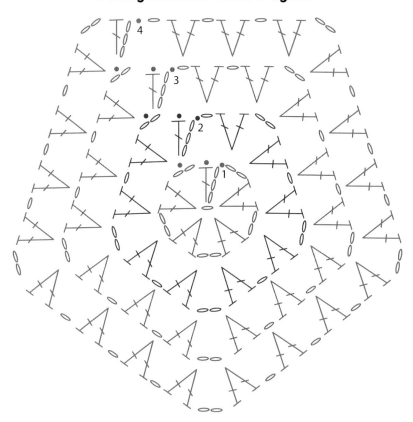

Neck Roll Pillow

This pillow cover begins with a tube of tiny shell stitches, joined after each round is complete. The end caps of the tube are created separately and worked in joined rounds of single crochet stitches. Slip stitches are used to join the end caps to each opening of the tube to complete.

YARN
Caron Cotton Cakes, Medium weight #4 (60% cotton + 40% acrylic; 530 yd./485 m; 8.8 oz/250 g cake):
- Cream: 1 cake (about 400 yd./365.76 g needed)

Also try: Loops & Threads Capri, Bernat Softee Cotton, Knit Picks Comfy Worsted

HOOK & OTHER MATERIALS
- US size G-6 (4.0 mm) crochet hook
- 14 in. x 5 in. (35.56 cm x 12.7 cm) neck roll pillow form
- Scissors
- Yarn needle
- Measuring tape
- Stitch markers

GAUGE
14.75 pattern sts = 4 in. (10.16 cm), 10 pattern rows = 4 in. (10.16 cm)
12 sc sts = 2.5 in. (6.35 cm), 12 sc rows = 2.75 in. (6.99 cm)

STITCH KEY
ch = chain
sc = single crochet
sl st = slip stitch
dc = double crochet

NOTE
Pattern worked in two parts: Pillow Sleeve (joined rounds, tube) and End Cap (joined rounds, center out).

Tip: Your stitch gauge is important for this project, because the tube you create should be about the same size as the pillow form you use. However, other fiber types and colors can be chosen to fit your taste!

SIZE/FINISHED MEASUREMENTS
One size: 20 in. around x 14.5 in. long (50.80 cm x 36.83 cm)

■ INSTRUCTIONS

Pillow Sleeve

Ch 72, sl st to join.

Round 1 (right side): Ch 1 (not a st, here and throughout), [sc, skip 1 st, work 3 dc into next st, skip 1 st] 18 times, sl st into top of first sc to join—72 sts; 18 sc + 54 dc.

Round 2: Ch 3 (first dc, here and throughout), dc into same st, [skip 1 st, sc, skip 1 st, work 3 dc into next st] 17 times, skip 1 st, sc, skip 1 st, dc into first st of round, sl st into top of first dc to join—72 sts; 18 sc + 54 dc.

Repeat Rounds 1 and 2 until 35 rounds complete (ending on a Round 1 repeat), fasten off.

End Cap (make 2)

Round 1 (right side): Ch 2 (not a st, here and throughout), work 6 sc into second ch from hook, sl st into top of first sc to join—6 sc.

Round 2: Ch 1, work 2 sc into each st around, sl st into top of first sc to join—12 sc.

Round 3: Ch 1, [sc into 1 st, work 2 sc into following st] 6 times, sl st into top of first sc to join—18 sc.

Round 4: Ch 1, [sc into 2 sts, work 2 sc into following st] 6 times, sl st into top of first sc to join—24 sc.

Round 5: Ch 1, [sc into 3 sts, work 2 sc into following st] 6 times, sl st into top of first sc to join—30 sc.

Round 6: Ch 1, [sc into 4 sts, work 2 sc into following st] 6 times, sl st into top of first sc to join—36 sc.

Round 7: Ch 1, [sc into 5 sts, work 2 sc into following st] 6 times, sl st into top of first sc to join—42 sc.

Neck Roll Pillow Sleeve Stitch Diagram

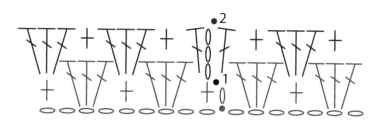

Stitch diagram not to full pattern scale.

Stitch Key

○ Chain

● Slip Stitch

+ Single Crochet

┬ Double Crochet

Round 8: Ch 1, [sc into 6 sts, work 2 sc into following st] 6 times, sl st into top of first sc to join—48 sc.
Round 9: Ch 1, [sc into 7 sts, work 2 sc into following st] 6 times, sl st into top of first sc to join—54 sc.
Round 10: Ch 1, [sc into 8 sts, work 2 sc into following st] 6 times, sl st into top of first sc to join—60 sc.
Round 11: Ch 1, [sc into 9 sts, work 2 sc into following st] 6 times, sl st into top of first sc to join—66 sc.
Round 12: Ch 1, [sc into 10 sts, work 2 sc into following st] 6 times, sl st into top of first sc to join—72 sc.
Do not fasten off; continue on to Finishing instructions.

Finishing

Ensure right side of Pillow Sleeve and End Cap are facing outward.
Hold Pillow Sleeve Round 1 together with Round 12 of first End Cap, sl st evenly around both thicknesses. Fasten off.
Insert pillow form into Pillow Sleeve.
Ensure right side of second End Cap is facing outward.
Hold Pillow Sleeve Round 35 together with Round 12 of second End Cap, sl st evenly around both thicknesses. Fasten off.
Sew in all yarn ends; trim excess.

Stitch Key

⬭ Chain

● Slip Stitch

+ Single Crochet

⋀ 2 Single Crochet into 1 Stitch

Neck Roll Pillow End Cap Stitch Diagram

Stitch diagram not to full pattern scale.

conclusion

Welcome to the world of crochet! You are now ready to venture out and find patterns that you love, using the skills you've learned here to make anything you want!

Get started on your next crochet project with one of these great titles, found anywhere books are sold:

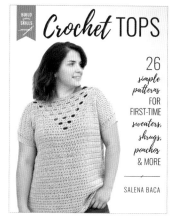
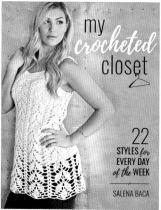

contributors

MATERIALS

Knit Picks
knitpicks.com

Lion Brand Yarn
lionbrand.com

Bernat, Caron, Patons, Red Heart Yarns
yarnspirations.com

Cascade Yarns
cascadeyarns.com

PATTERN TESTING

- Rachel Anne
- Amanda Dodge
- Jaime Grey
- Courtney Knorr-Warriner
- Amy McKeever
- Tammy Peters
- Jackie Ramsdell
- Amanda Woodbury
- Linda Woodthorpe
- Michelle Wulf
- Laurie Yuenger

PHOTOS

- Tutorial Photography: Salena Baca
- Product Photography: Julie Lynn Photography

resources

Some crochet stitches and techniques are best learned when you watch a video while following written definitions and text. Please visit these resources for an assortment of crochet knowledge and tutorials:

YarnSub.com
A free site where yarn substitution is made easy!

YouTube.com/AmericanCrochetAssociation
A free library of video tutorials for crochet stitches and other basics like holding your yarn and hook, slipknot, slip stitch, color changes, weaving and sewing in ends, and much more!

Ravelry.com/designers/salena-baca
Got a question about one of these designs, or just want to see how others have worked them up? You can find this book, and all the designs, neatly listed on Ravelry with direct access to Salena Baca!

index of stitches and techniques